D0782287

Information Security Policy Development for Compliance

ISO/IEC 27001, NIST SP 800-53,
HIPAA Standard, PCI DSS V2.0,
and AUP V5.0

OTHER INFORMATION SECURITY BOOKS FROM AUERBACH

Asset Protection through Security Awareness
Tyler Justin Speed
ISBN 978-1-4398-0982-2

The CISO Handbook: A Practical Guide to Securing Your Company
Michael Gentile, Ron Collette, and Thomas D. August
ISBN 978-0-8493-1952-5

CISO's Guide to Penetration Testing: A Framework to Plan, Manage, and Maximize Benefits
James S. Tiller
ISBN 978-1-4398-8027-2

The Complete Book of Data Anonymization: From Planning to Implementation
Balaji Raghunathan
ISBN 978-1-4398-7730-2

Cybersecurity: Public Sector Threats and Responses
Kim J. Andreasson, Editor
ISBN 9781-4398-4663-6

Cyber Security Essentials
James Graham, Editor
ISBN 978-1-4398-5123-4

Cybersecurity for Industrial Control Systems: SCADA, DCS, PLC, HMI, and SIS
Tyson Macaulay and Bryan L. Singer
ISBN 978-1-4398-0196-3

Cyberspace and Cybersecurity
George Kostopoulos Request
ISBN 978-1-4665-0133-1

Defense Against the Black Arts: How Hackers Do What They Do and How to Protect against It
Jesse Varsalone and Matthew McFadden
ISBN 978-1-4398-2119-0

The Definitive Guide to Complying with the HIPAA/HITECH Privacy and Security Rules
John J. Trinckes, Jr.
ISBN 978-1-4665-0767-8

Digital Forensics Explained
Greg Gogolin
ISBN 978-1-4398-7495-0

Digital Forensics for Handheld Devices
Eamon P. Doherty
ISBN 978-1-4398-9877-2

Electronically Stored Information: The Complete Guide to Management, Understanding, Acquisition, Storage, Search, and Retrieval
David R. Matthews
ISBN 978-1-4398-7726-5

FISMA Principles and Best Practices: Beyond Compliance
Patrick D. Howard
ISBN 978-1-4200-7829-9

Information Security Governance Simplified: From the Boardroom to the Keyboard
Todd Fitzgerald
ISBN 978-1-4398-1163-4

Information Technology Control and Audit, Fourth Edition
Sandra Senft, Frederick Gallegos, and Aleksandra Davis
ISBN 978-1-4398-9320-3

Managing the Insider Threat: No Dark Corners
Nick Catrantzos
ISBN 978-1-4398-7292-5

Network Attacks and Defenses: A Hands-on Approach
Zouheir Trabelsi, Kadhim Hayawi, Arwa Al Braiki, and Sujith Samuel Mathew
ISBN 978-1-4665-1794-3

PRAGMATIC Security Metrics: Applying Metametrics to Information Security
W. Krag Brotby and Gary Hinson
ISBN 978-1-4398-8152-1

The Security Risk Assessment Handbook: A Complete Guide for Performing Security Risk Assessments, Second Edition
Douglas Landoll
ISBN 978-1-4398-2148-0

The 7 Qualities of Highly Secure Software
Mano Paul
ISBN 978-1-4398-1446-8

Smart Grid Security: An End-to-End View of Security in the New Electrical Grid
Gilbert N. Sorebo and Michael C. Echols
ISBN 978-1-4398-5587-4

Windows Networking Tools: The Complete Guide to Management, Troubleshooting, and Security
Gilbert Held
ISBN 978-1-4665-1106-4

AUERBACH PUBLICATIONS
www.auerbach-publications.com
To Order Call: 1-800-272-7737 • Fax: 1-800-374-3401
E-mail: orders@crcpress.com

Information Security Policy Development for Compliance

ISO/IEC 27001, NIST SP 800-53, HIPAA Standard, PCI DSS V2.0, and AUP V5.0

Barry L. Williams

CRC Press
Taylor & Francis Group
Boca Raton   London   New York

CRC Press is an imprint of the
Taylor & Francis Group, an **informa** business
AN AUERBACH BOOK

CRC Press
Taylor & Francis Group
6000 Broken Sound Parkway NW, Suite 300
Boca Raton, FL 33487-2742

© 2013 by Taylor & Francis Group, LLC
CRC Press is an imprint of Taylor & Francis Group, an Informa business

No claim to original U.S. Government works

Printed on acid-free paper
Version Date: 20130118

International Standard Book Number-13: 978-1-4665-8058-9 (Hardback)

This book contains information obtained from authentic and highly regarded sources. Reasonable efforts have been made to publish reliable data and information, but the author and publisher cannot assume responsibility for the validity of all materials or the consequences of their use. The authors and publishers have attempted to trace the copyright holders of all material reproduced in this publication and apologize to copyright holders if permission to publish in this form has not been obtained. If any copyright material has not been acknowledged please write and let us know so we may rectify in any future reprint.

Except as permitted under U.S. Copyright Law, no part of this book may be reprinted, reproduced, transmitted, or utilized in any form by any electronic, mechanical, or other means, now known or hereafter invented, including photocopying, microfilming, and recording, or in any information storage or retrieval system, without written permission from the publishers.

For permission to photocopy or use material electronically from this work, please access www.copyright.com (http://www.copyright.com/) or contact the Copyright Clearance Center, Inc. (CCC), 222 Rosewood Drive, Danvers, MA 01923, 978-750-8400. CCC is a not-for-profit organization that provides licenses and registration for a variety of users. For organizations that have been granted a photocopy license by the CCC, a separate system of payment has been arranged.

Trademark Notice: Product or corporate names may be trademarks or registered trademarks, and are used only for identification and explanation without intent to infringe.

Library of Congress Cataloging-in-Publication Data

Williams, Barry L.
    Information security policy development for compliance : ISO/IEC 27001, NIST SP 800-53, HIPAA standard, PCI DSS V2.0, and AUP V5.0 / Barry L. Williams.
        p. cm.
    ISBN 978-1-4665-8058-9 (alk. paper)
    1. Computer security. 2. Computer networks--Security measures. 3. Data protection. 4. Access control. I. Title.

QA76.9.A25.W5495 2013
005.8--dc23   2012042439

Visit the Taylor & Francis Web site at
http://www.taylorandfrancis.com

and the CRC Press Web site at
http://www.crcpress.com

Contents

Introduction

Operational necessity dictates the majority of actions taken by an IT department. Both documented and undocumented policies and procedures are developed to support the performance of actions dictated by such operational necessity. However, these are not the only reasons for policy development. Informational resources must be protected from unauthorized access. A fully developed information security program with documented security policies and procedures provides the structure and guidance needed to help ensure the protection of informational resources.

To summarize, we can say that an information security policy is written to protect the organization's data and define management's strategy for securing sensitive data. Management must be actively involved in providing input, as well as in the review and approval of all policy documents.

There are many freely available templates and examples of security policies on the Internet. I have reviewed dozens of approved organizational information security policies that were obviously lifted from various sites or borrowed from other organizations. Much of this comes from the sudden need to comply quickly with a regulatory requirement or a certain compliance standard (more on this shortly). This is very upsetting to the true security professional. I doubt that management would develop its strategic business plan by copying the plan of a competitor or an organization from a different industry. So why would anyone expect the security plan for one organization to be applicable to his or her own environment?

In order to prevent myself from going on a tirade, I will concentrate on explaining my thoughts on security policy development. The goal is to elicit from management opinions on information security and to document the current procedures in place, formal and informal. The purpose of this book is to provide a methodology to facilitate the elicitation process. By asking pointed questions concerning specific subjects, the elicitor can obtain the information needed to write a relevant policy. More importantly, this methodology can help the elicitor to determine what security issues exist and the weaknesses and vulnerabilities of the organization. This goes hand in hand with a formal risk assessment (RA), but is beyond the scope of this writing. However, RA procedures are covered in the body of this document.

I mentioned compliance standards requirements earlier. Many policies are written to comply with a certain regulation or standard. What should be obvious, but is often overlooked, is the fact that what is stated in a policy should accurately reflect what is happening in the organization's environment. For example, if the policy states a requirement to review firewall and router rule sets at least every 6 months in order to comply with the PCI Data Security Standard 1.1.6, the organization must be able to demonstrate that such reviews are taking place. Otherwise, the policy means little because the auditor is going to note that the organization is "not compliant" for that requirement if no documentation of such a review exists.

Compliance standards, of which there are many, can be and should be used as a guide to write comprehensive and effective security policies. Many standards cover much of the same topics, but state the requirements in a slightly different way. It is helpful to see what each standard says about the various security topics; however, wading through the morass can be very time consuming. The structure and use of hyperlinks in the e-book version are designed to facilitate your research of the various standards. Some of the standards with which I am familiar follow:

- ISO/IEC 27001 (Appendix A). This standard is a specification for an information security management system (ISMS). Appendix A catalogs a wide range of controls and other measures relevant to information security.
- PCI DSS V2.0. This security standard is intended to help organizations protect cardholder information (i.e., credit card account information). Organizations that process, store, or transmit cardholder data are required to be compliant with this standard.
- AUP V5.0. The agreed upon procedures were created for independent accounting and assessment firms. The AUP is used to evaluate service provider security, privacy, and business continuity controls.
- HIPAA Security Rule. This rule establishes standards to protect electronic personal health information (ePHI) that is created, received, used, or maintained by a covered entity.
- NIST SP 800-53. This government publication provides guidelines for selecting and specifying security controls for information systems supporting the executive agencies of the federal government. Many organizations in private industry use NIST SP 800-53 as a guide for their own security management.

This is not a comprehensive list of standards, but let us stop here and organize our thoughts. Our goal is to write a comprehensive security policy that meets the security needs of the organization using the compliance standards as a guide to ensure that our security policy meets the requirements of the various standards. In that regard, the statements that follow are designed to elicit responses from management in order to write an information security policy document that incorporates the requirements from the various standards.

What makes the e-book version unique is the hyperlinks beside each statement. You should use the links to see what the various standards say concerning each topic. The links will provide explanation and guidance in determining what the policy should include.

Unfortunately, there are a couple of caveats. Please note that not all the standards requirements listed in this document are linked, although we believe that all the key controls are addressed. However, this will depend on your specific environment and you may need to cover other requirements in your policies. Also, in certain instances, the links may provide a loose relationship among the various standards. There is not always a one-to-one correspondence to the different control standards.

Although I have never seen this done, I recommend including references to the control requirements throughout your policy documentation. Won't the auditors be impressed!

There are no templates here. No fill-in the blanks. Security policies should be written based on the uniqueness of each operational environment. This document is meant to serve as a guide for security policy development. I hope this helps!

If you have any questions, please contact me through my website: www.williamsitaudit.com.

Entity-Level Policies and Procedures
Information Security Policy Management

	Describe management's commitment to develop and maintain formal, documented, and approved information security policies and procedures that encompass information values, information protection, and an overall organizational commitment.	ISO/IEC 27001	A.5.1.1
			A.6.1.1
		NIST SP 800-53	PS-1
		HIPAA Standard	164.316(a)
		PCI DSS V2.0	12.1 thru 12.9.6
		AUP V5.0	B.1
	Define the individual or group assigned the responsibility of ensuring that the information security policy is regularly reviewed, documented, and approved. This assignment should be defined in the overall security policy.	ISO/IEC 27001	A.6.1.3
		NIST SP 800-53	PM-2
		HIPAA Standard	164.308(a)(2)
		PCI DSS V2.0	12.5
		AUP V5.0	B.2
	Describe the security policy review and approval process.	ISO/IEC 27001	A.5.1.2
		NIST SP 800-53	
		HIPAA Standard	164.316(a)
		PCI DSS V2.0	12.1.3
			12.3
		AUP V5.0	B.2
	Define the frequency of the security policy review (annually at a minimum) to ensure its continuing stability, adequacy, and effectiveness.	ISO/IEC 27001	A.5.1.2
		NIST SP 800-53	
		HIPAA Standard	164.316(b)(2)(iii)
		PCI DSS V2.0	12.1.3
		AUP V5.0	B.2
	Describe how the security policy document is communicated to all employees (e.g., upon hire, annual awareness training, or intranet).	ISO/IEC 27001	A.5.1.1
		NIST SP 800-53	
		HIPAA Standard	
		PCI DSS V2.0	12.1
		AUP V5.0	B.1
	Describe management's intent and support of the goals and principles of information security.	ISO/IEC 27001	A.6.1.1
		NIST SP 800-53	PM-2
		HIPAA Standard	
		PCI DSS V2.0	
		AUP V5.0	
	Define the compliance requirements (legislative, regulatory, and contractual requirements) that the information security policy is designed to address.	ISO/IEC 27001	A.15.1.1
		NIST SP 800-53	IA-7
		HIPAA Standard	
		PCI DSS V2.0	
		AUP V5.02	

continued

Information Security Policy Management (continued)

Define the security education, training, and awareness requirements for every employee and contractor with access to the organization's information resources.	ISO/IEC 27001	A.8.2.2	
	NIST SP 800-53	AT-2	
		AT-3	
		IR-2	
	HIPAA Standard	164.308(a)(5)(i)	
	PCI DSS V2.0	12.6	
	AUP V5.0		
Describe the formal sanction process for personnel failing to comply with the organization's information security policies and procedures.	ISO/IEC 27001	A.8.2.3	
	NIST SP 800-53	PS-8	
	HIPAA Standard		
	PCI DSS V2.0		
	AUP V5.0		
If applicable, describe the use of a cross-functional group of management representatives (e.g., a steering committee) from relevant parts of the organization to coordinate the implementation of information security controls.	ISO/IEC 27001	A.6.1.2	
	NIST SP 800-53	PL-1	
	HIPAA Standard		
	PCI DSS V2.0		
	AUP V5.0		
Describe how management approves assignment of specific roles and responsibilities for information security across the organization.	ISO/IEC 27001	A.6.1.3	
		A.8.1.1	
	NIST SP 800-53	PM-2	
	HIPAA Standard		
	PCI DSS V2.0		
	AUP V5.0		
Describe how appropriate contacts with special interest groups or other specialist security forums and professional associations are maintained. Management should support such associations and memberships as a matter of policy.	ISO/IEC 27001	A.6.1.7	
	NIST SP 800-53	AT-5	
	HIPAA Standard		
	PCI DSS V2.0		
	AUP V5.0		
Describe the use of independent, outside organizations to periodically review the organization's approach to managing information security and its implementation.	ISO/IEC 27001	A.6.1.8	
	NIST SP 800-53	CA-7(1)	
	HIPAA Standard	164.308(a)(8)	
	PCI DSS V2.0		
	AUP V5.0		
Describe the organization's risk assessment (RA) and risk management process. Output from the assessment should include a formal RA document that is submitted to management for review.	ISO/IEC 27001	A.14.1.2	
	NIST SP 800-53	RA-1	
	HIPAA Standard	164.308(a)(1)(ii)(A)	
	PCI DSS V2.0	12.1.2	
		12.1.3	
	AUP V5.0	A.1	
		A.2	

Information Security Policy Management (continued)

Define the information security roles and responsibilities to include each of the following: • Responsibility for creating and distributing security policies and procedures • Responsibility for monitoring and analyzing security alerts and distributing information to appropriate information security and business unit management personnel. • Responsibility for creating and distributing security incident response and escalation procedures. • Responsibility for administering user account and authentication management. • Responsibility for monitoring and controlling access to data.	ISO/IEC 27001	A.8.1.1
	NIST SP 800-53	PS-2
	HIPAA Standard	
	PCI DSS V2.0	
	AUP V5.0	

Human Resources Security

Describe the on-boarding and ongoing security awareness education and training provided to employees and contractors.	ISO/IEC 27001	A.8.2.2
	NIST SP 800-53	AT-2
		AT-3
	HIPAA Standard	
	PCI DSS V2.0	12.6
		12.6.1
		12.6.2
	AUP V5.0	E.1
Describe the application design and related security awareness training provided to developers annually.	ISO/IEC 27001	
	NIST SP 800-53	
	HIPAA Standard	
	PCI DSS V2.0	
	AUP V5.0	I.9
		I.10
Describe the frequency and method of acknowledgment of the various types of security awareness training described above.	ISO/IEC 27001	A.8.2.2
	NIST SP 800-53	AT-2
		AT-3
	HIPAA Standard	
	PCI DSS V2.0	
	AUP V5.0	E.1

continued

Human Resources Security (continued)

Describe the controls in place that govern how security roles and responsibilities for individuals not engaged via the organization's employment process (e.g., engaged via a third-party organization) are clearly defined and communicated.	ISO/IEC 27001	A.6.2.3
		A.8.1.1
		A.8.2.1
	NIST SP 800-53	PS-7
	HIPAA Standard	
	PCI DSS V2.0	
	AUP V5.0	
Define forms and documents, including acknowledgments, used in the on-boarding process. For example: • Security policy • Acceptable use policy • Nondisclosure agreement • Completion of security awareness training Describe how employees acknowledge their understanding and acceptance of the above.	ISO/IEC 27001	A.6.1.5
		A.8.1.3
	NIST SP 800-53	AT-4
	HIPAA Standard	
	PCI DSS V2.0	
	AUP V5.0	B.3
		C.1
Describe the process for giving timely performance evaluations against individual objectives derived from the organization's goals, established standards, and specific job responsibilities.	ISO/IEC 27001	
	NIST SP 800-53	
	HIPAA Standard	
	PCI DSS V2.0	
	AUP V5.0	
Define the requirement that documented job descriptions for all critical positions be maintained.	ISO/IEC 27001	A.8.1
	NIST SP 800-53	
	HIPAA Standard	
	PCI DSS V2.0	
	AUP V5.0	
Describe the organization's process and responsibilities for terminating employment and revoking the access to information systems. Define any documents or forms used in this process, including e-mail communications.	ISO/IEC 27001	A.8.3.1
		A.8.3.2
	NIST SP 800-53	PS-4
		PS-5
	HIPAA Standard	164.308(a)(3)(ii)(C)
	PCI DSS V2.0	
	AUP V5.0	
Describe the process that ensures that all employees, contractors, and third-party users surrender all of the organization's assets in their possession upon termination of their employment, contract, or agreement.	ISO/IEC 27001	A.8.3.2
	NIST SP 800-53	PS-4
	HIPAA Standard	
	PCI DSS V2.0	
	AUP V5.0	

Human Resources Security (continued)

	Define the information security roles and responsibilities to include each of the following: • Responsibility for creating and distributing security policies and procedures • Responsibility for monitoring and analyzing security alerts and distributing information to appropriate information security and business unit management personnel. • Responsibility for creating and distributing security incident response and escalation procedures. • Responsibility for administering user account and authentication management. • Responsibility for monitoring and controlling access to data.	ISO/IEC 27001	A.8.1.1
		NIST SP 800-53	PS-2
		HIPAA Standard	
		PCI DSS V2.0	
		AUP V5.0	
	Define the requirement that employee background checks include the following: • Criminal history • Credit check • Reference check • Work history check Describe other types of background checks if appropriate.	ISO/IEC 27001	A.8.1.2
		NIST SP 800-53	PS-3
		HIPAA Standard	
		PCI DSS V2.0	
		AUP V5.0	E.2
	Describe the disciplinary process for employees who have committed a security breach.	ISO/IEC 27001	A.8.2.3
		NIST SP 800-53	PS-8
		HIPAA Standard	164.308(a)(1)(ii)(C)
		PCI DSS V2.0	
		AUP V5.0	

Acceptable Use

	Describe the acceptable and nonacceptable uses of the organization's resources.	ISO/IEC 27001	A.7.1.3
		NIST SP 800-53	PL-4
		HIPAA Standard	
		PCI DSS V2.0	
		AUP V5.0	

continued

Acceptable Use (continued)

	Describe appropriate and nonappropriate use of resources to include the following: • Appropriate use of e-mail and related resources • No expectation of privacy • Monitoring and logging with or without the user's consent NOTE: The above may be included as part of the overall information security policy. List other acceptable and nonacceptable uses for your organization.	ISO/IEC 27001	A.7.1.3
		NIST SP 800-53	PL-4
		HIPAA Standard	
		PCI DSS V2.0	
		AUP V5.0	

Data Classification and Document Retention

	Describe the method of information classification.	ISO/IEC 27001	A.7.2.1
		NIST SP 800-53	RA-2
		HIPAA Standard	
		PCI DSS V2.0	
		AUP V5.0	P.1
	Describe the procedures for information labeling and handling performed in accordance with the information classification scheme.	ISO/IEC 27001	A.7.2.2
		NIST SP 800-53	AC-16
		HIPAA Standard	
		PCI DSS V2.0	9.7.1
		AUP V5.0	
	Are data and sensitive documents maintained according to applicable laws and regulations? Define any laws or regulations that apply.	ISO/IEC 27001	
		NIST SP 800-53	
		HIPAA Standard	164.316(b)(2)(i)
		PCI DSS V2.0	3.1.1
			3.2
		AUP V5.0	

Regulatory Compliance

	Describe and list the regulatory agencies and associated regulations, if any, that apply to the organization's business environment (e.g., GLBA, HIPAA, SOX, PCI, FISMA, FDCPA).	ISO/IEC 27001	A.15.1.1
		NIST SP 800-53	
		HIPAA Standard	
		PCI DSS V2.0	
		AUP V5.0	
	Describe the guidelines that define the legal use of software and other intellectual property.	ISO/IEC 27001	A.15.1.2
		NIST SP 800-53	SA-6
		HIPAA Standard	
		PCI DSS V2.0	
		AUP V5.0	

Regulatory Compliance (continued)

Define the frequency and describe the use of internal personnel and/or third-party organizations to provide security reviews, security assessments, vulnerability scans, and penetration tests.	ISO/IEC 27001	A.15.2.2
	NIST SP 800-53	CA-2
		RA-5
	HIPAA Standard	
	PCI DSS V2.0	11.2
		11.3
	AUP V5.0	I.1
		I.8
		L.2

Physical and Environmental Security

Describe the physical procedures the organization has developed to facilitate the implementation of physical and environmental protection controls.	ISO/IEC 27001	A.9.1
	NIST SP 800-53	PE-1
	HIPAA Standard	164.310(a)(2)(ii)
	PCI DSS V2.0	
	AUP V5.0	
Describe the procedures in place to perform periodic compliance audits of the organization's physical security environment.	ISO/IEC 27001	
	NIST SP 800-53	
	HIPAA Standard	
	PCI DSS V2.0	
	AUP V5.0	F.6
Describe the use of security perimeters and/or physical security used to protect areas that contain information facilities.	ISO/IEC 27001	A.9.1.1
	NIST SP 800-53	PE-3
	HIPAA Standard	164.310(a)(1)
	PCI DSS V2.0	
	AUP V5.0	F.2
		F.4
Describe the controls in place to approve, register, and supervise visitors to the organization's facilities.	ISO/IEC 27001	A.9.1.2
	NIST SP 800-53	PE-7
	HIPAA Standard	
	PCI DSS V2.0	9.4
	AUP V5.0	F.4
Describe the use of visible identification for employees, contractors, third-party users, and visitors.	ISO/IEC 27001	A.9.1.2
	NIST SP 800-53	
	HIPAA Standard	
	PCI DSS V2.0	9.2
		9.3.2
	AUP V5.0	F.4

continued

Physical and Environmental Security (continued)

	Describe the physical protection employed by the organization against damage from fire, flood, earthquake, explosion, civil unrest, and other forms of natural or man-made disasters.	ISO/IEC 27001	A.9.1.4
		NIST SP 800-53	PE-13
			PE-14
			PE-15
		HIPAA Standard	
		PCI DSS V2.0	
		AUP V5.0	F.1
	Describe the type of fire detection and/or fire suppression in use inside the data center and other facilities.	ISO/IEC 27001	A.9.1.4
		NIST SP 800-53	PE-13
		HIPAA Standard	
		PCI DSS V2.0	
		AUP V5.0	F.1
	Describe procedures that ensure the organization employs physical information system security controls at alternate work sites during a disaster recovery mode of operation.	ISO/IEC 27001	A.9.2.5
		NIST SP 800-53	PE-17
		HIPAA Standard	164.310(a)(2)(i)
		PCI DSS V2.0	
		AUP V5.0	
	Describe the information system maintenance procedures that document repairs and modifications to the facility components related to physical security.	ISO/IEC 27001	
		NIST SP 800-53	MA-1
		HIPAA Standard	164.310(a)(2)(iv)
		PCI DSS V2.0	
		AUP V5.0	
	Describe the type of climate control systems utilized, especially for data centers and server, network, or telecommunications rooms.	ISO/IEC 27001	
		NIST SP 800-53	PE-14
		HIPAA Standard	
		PCI DSS V2.0	
		AUP V5.0	F.1
	Describe the physical controls of delivery and loading areas that restrict access from those areas to other facilities.	ISO/IEC 27001	A.9.1.6
		NIST SP 800-53	PE-3
			PE-16
		HIPAA Standard	
		PCI DSS V2.0	
		AUP V5.0	F.4
	Describe the physical security controls for computer rooms, data centers, and other sensitive environments.	ISO/IEC 27001	A.9.1.2
		NIST SP 800-53	PE-3
			PE-6
			PE-7
		HIPAA Standard	
		PCI DSS V2.0	
		AUP V5.0	F.2
			F.4

Physical and Environmental Security (continued)

Describe the use of video monitoring systems and other access-control mechanisms in place to monitor individual physical access. Define how long video recordings are retained.	ISO/IEC 27001	A.9.1.5	
	NIST SP 800-53		
	HIPAA Standard		
	PCI DSS V2.0	9.1.1	
	AUP V5.0		
Describe how physical access to publicly accessible network jacks is restricted.	ISO/IEC 27001		
	NIST SP 800-53		
	HIPAA Standard		
	PCI DSS V2.0	9.1.2	
	AUP V5.0		
Describe how physical access to wireless access points, gateways, and handheld devices is appropriately restricted.	ISO/IEC 27001	A.9.2.1	
	NIST SP 800-53	PE-18	
	HIPAA Standard		
	PCI DSS V2.0	9.1.3	
	AUP V5.0		
Describe procedures for assigning badges to employees and visitors, including granting new badges, changing access requirements, and revoking terminated employee and visitor expired badges.	ISO/IEC 27001		
	NIST SP 800-53	PE-7	
	HIPAA Standard	164.310(a)(2)(iii)	
	PCI DSS V2.0	9.3	
	AUP V5.0	F.4	
		F.5	
		H.7	
Describe the appropriate use of workstations and the appropriate physical surroundings and physical safeguards of workstations that can access sensitive information.	ISO/IEC 27001	A.9.1.3	
		A.11.3.2	
	NIST SP 800-53	PE-5	
	HIPAA Standard	164.310(b)	
	PCI DSS V2.0		
	AUP V5.0	F.3	
Describe any policies and guidelines designed and implemented for working in areas that can access sensitive information. This may include the prohibition of the use or presence of photographic, video, audio, or other recording equipment, including cell phones.	ISO/IEC 27001	A.9.1.5	
	NIST SP 800-53	PL-4	
	HIPAA Standard	164.310(c)	
	PCI DSS V2.0		
	AUP V5.0	F.3	

Access-Control Policies and Procedures

Logical Access

Describe the user registration and deregistration procedure (provisioning and revocation) for granting access to information systems.	ISO/IEC 27001	A.11.2.1
	NIST SP 800-53	AC-1
	HIPAA Standard	164.308(a)(3)(ii)(A)
		164.308(a)(4)(i)
		164.308(a)(4)(ii)(B)
	PCI DSS V2.0	7.1.3
		8.5.4
	AUP V5.0	H.2
		H.5
Describe procedures to modify a user's access rights—for example, when a user transfers to a new position with different job responsibilities.	ISO/IEC 27001	A.11.2.1
	NIST SP 800-53	AC-2
	HIPAA Standard	164.308(a)(4)(ii)(C)
	PCI DSS V2.0	8.5.1
	AUP V5.0	
Describe how users are assigned access rights to operating systems and applications based on their job requirements.	ISO/IEC 27001	A.11.2.2
	NIST SP 800-53	AC-6
	HIPAA Standard	164.308(a)(3)(ii)(A)
		164.308(a)(3)(ii)(B)
	PCI DSS V2.0	7.1.2
	AUP V5.0	H.3
Describe how original, unique passwords are disseminated to users and that the system requires the password to be changed upon first use.	ISO/IEC 27001	A.11.3.1
	NIST SP 800-53	IA-5
	HIPAA Standard	164.308(a)(5)(ii)(D)
	PCI DSS V2.0	8.1
		8.5.3
	AUP V5.0	
Define the frequency, annually at a minimum, of management's review of user access.	ISO/IEC 27001	A.11.2.4
	NIST SP 800-53	AC-2
	HIPAA Standard	
	PCI DSS V2.0	
	AUP V5.0	
Describe the process used by IT and business management (i.e., the data owners) to periodically review the rights and privileges assigned to users and the procedure used to report and correct noted discrepancies.	ISO/IEC 27001	A.11.2.4
	NIST SP 800-53	AC-2
	HIPAA Standard	164.308(a)(1)(ii)(D)
		164.308(a)(3)(ii)(B)
	PCI DSS V2.0	
	AUP V5.0	

Logical Access (continued)

Define the requirement that the system displays a security banner during boot-up that provides a general notice warning that the system should only be accessed by authorized users.	ISO/IEC 27001	A.15.1.5
	NIST SP 800-53	AC-8
	HIPAA Standard	
	PCI DSS V2.0	
	AUP V5.0	L.1
Define the use of unique user IDs and passwords for general users, network administrators, system programmers, and database administrators.	ISO/IEC 27001	A.11.5.2
	NIST SP 800-53	IA-2
	HIPAA Standard	164.312(a)(2)(i)
	PCI DSS V2.0	8.1
		10.1
	AUP V5.0	
Describe any exceptions to the above. For example, a general terminal or workstation with appropriately limited access on the shop floor may be required as an operational necessity.	ISO/IEC 27001	A.11.5.2
	NIST SP 800-53	IA-2
	HIPAA Standard	
	PCI DSS V2.0	8.5.8
	AUP V5.0	
Define the organization's clear desk and clear screen policy and procedures. This may be included as a section in the overall security policy document.	ISO/IEC 27001	A.11.3.3
	NIST SP 800-53	AC-11
	HIPAA Standard	
	PCI DSS V2.0	
	AUP V5.0	
Describe how the organization ensures that access rights are assigned to enforce segregation of duties and the principle of least privilege.	ISO/IEC 27001	A.11.2.2
	NIST SP 800-53	AC-5
		AC-6
	HIPAA Standard	164.308(a)(3)(i)
	PCI DSS V2.0	7.1.1
	AUP V5.0	
Describe how authentication is performed for access to any database containing sensitive information. This includes access by applications, administrators, and all other users. Describe how direct access or queries to databases are restricted to database administrators.	ISO/IEC 27001	A.11.6.1
	NIST SP 800-53	
	HIPAA Standard	
	PCI DSS V2.0	8.5.16
	AUP V5.0	
Describe how two-factor authentication is implemented for remote access to the network by employees, administrators, and third parties.	ISO/IEC 27001	A.11.4.2
	NIST SP 800-53	
	HIPAA Standard	
	PCI DSS V2.0	8.3
	AUP V5.0	

Password Management

Describe the password controls in place for operating systems and access to critical applications. Typical password control parameters include: • Password complexity • Minimum password length • Maximum password age • Minimum password age • Password history • Account lockout after a specified number of unsuccessful log-on attempts Describe other password parameters used at your organization for all operating systems and applications, if applicable.	ISO/IEC 27001	A.11.2.3
		A.11.5.3
	NIST SP 800-53	IA-5
	HIPAA Standard	164.308(a)(5)(ii)(D)
	PCI DSS V2.0	8.5.9
		8.5.10
		8.5.11
		8.5.12
		8.5.13
		8.5.14
	AUP V5.0	H.1
Define the requirement that all passwords must be rendered unreadable during transmission and storage on all system components, using strong cryptography.	ISO/IEC 27001	
	NIST SP 800-53	IA-5
	HIPAA Standard	
	PCI DSS V2.0	8.4
	AUP V5.0	
Describe how users are identified before performing password resets.	ISO/IEC 27001	A.11.2.3
	NIST SP 800-53	
	HIPAA Standard	164.308(a)(5)(ii)(D)
	PCI DSS V2.0	8.5.2
	AUP V5.0	
Describe the use of strong authentication methods for sensitive environments (e.g., smart cards, tokens, or biometrics).	ISO/IEC 27001	
	NIST SP 800-53	IA-2
	HIPAA Standard	
	PCI DSS V2.0	8.2
		8.3
	AUP V5.0	
Define the use of screen and/or session locks after a period of inactivity.	ISO/IEC 27001	A.11.5.5
	NIST SP 800-53	AC-11
	HIPAA Standard	164.312(a)(2)(iii)
	PCI DSS V2.0	8.5.15
	AUP V5.0	H.5
Describe any policies and procedures in place to restrict connection times for high-risk applications.	ISO/IEC 27001	A.11.5.6
	NIST SP 800-53	
	HIPAA Standard	
	PCI DSS V2.0	
	AUP V5.0	H.5

Wireless, Mobile Computing, and Teleworking

Describe and define the acceptable configuration for wireless connections to the network.	ISO/IEC 27001	
	NIST SP 800-53	AC-18
	HIPAA Standard	
	PCI DSS V2.0	2.1.1
		4.1.1
	AUP V5.0	
Describe the acceptable (appropriate and inappropriate) uses of the wireless local area network (WLAN) environment.	ISO/IEC 27001	A.7.1.3
	NIST SP 800-53	
	HIPAA Standard	
	PCI DSS V2.0	12.3
	AUP V5.0	
Include in the policy the considerations made to secure access points: • Application of the latest firmware and patches • Changing of default passwords • Service set identification (SSID) not broadcast • Access points renamed from the manufacturer default Advanced encryption standard (AES) encryption employed with WPA2 encryption using a strong passphrase.	ISO/IEC 27001	
	NIST SP 800-53	
	HIPAA Standard	
	PCI DSS V2.0	2.1.1
		4.1.1
	AUP V5.0	
Define the requirement that perimeter firewalls must be installed between any wireless networks and other networks containing sensitive data. Describe how firewalls are configured to deny or control traffic from the wireless environment into networks containing sensitive data.	ISO/IEC 27001	A.11.4.5
	NIST SP 800-53	
	HIPAA Standard	
	PCI DSS V2.0	1.2.3
	AUP V5.0	
Describe the procedure to test for the presence of wireless access points and detect unauthorized wireless access points on a quarterly basis.	ISO/IEC 27001	
	NIST SP 800-53	AC-18
	HIPAA Standard	
	PCI DSS V2.0	11.1
	AUP V5.0	G.15
Define the organization's mobile computing procedures that include requirements for physical protection, access controls, cryptographic techniques, backups, and virus protection.	ISO/IEC 27001	A.11.7.1
	NIST SP 800-53	AC-19
	HIPAA Standard	
	PCI DSS V2.0	
	AUP V5.0	

continued

Wireless, Mobile Computing, and Teleworking (continued)

Define the teleworking activities authorized by management.	ISO/IEC 27001	A.11.7.2	
	NIST SP 800-53	AC-17	
	HIPAA Standard		
	PCI DSS V2.0		
	AUP V5.0		

Change Control and Change Management

Software Development

Describe how software applications (internal and external, including web-based administrative access to applications) are developed based on industry best practices. Describe how information security is incorporated throughout the software development life cycle (SDLC).	ISO/IEC 27001	A.12.1.1	
	NIST SP 800-53	SA-3	
	HIPAA Standard		
	PCI DSS V2.0	6.3	
	AUP V5.0	I.2	
		I.5	
		I.7	
Develop SDLC policy and procedures for the organization.	ISO/IEC 27001		
	NIST SP 800-53	CM-9	
		SA-3	
	HIPAA Standard		
	PCI DSS V2.0	6.3.1	
		6.3.2	
	AUP V5.0	I.5	
Define the requirement that web applications must be regularly tested to ensure that they are not vulnerable to the following: • Cross-site scripting (XSS) • Injection flaws, particularly structured query language (SQL) injection • Malicious file execution • Insecure direct object references • Cross-site request forger (CSFR) • Information leakage and improper error handling • Broken authentication and session management • Insecure cryptographic storage • Insecure communications Failure to restrict uniform resource locator (URL) access	ISO/IEC 27001	A.12.1.1	
	NIST SP 800-53		
	HIPAA Standard		
	PCI DSS V2.0	6.5	
	AUP V5.0	I.6	

Software Development (continued)

Describe the method for ensuring that public-facing web applications are protected against known attacks (e.g., reviewing public-facing web applications using an automated application vulnerability tool, etc.)	ISO/IEC 27001	A.12.6.1
	NIST SP 800-53	
	HIPAA Standard	
	PCI DSS V2.0	6.6
	AUP V5.0	I.1
Describe the data input validation checks performed by the organization's application(s).	ISO/IEC 27001	A.12.2.1
	NIST SP 800-53	SI-10
	HIPAA Standard	
	PCI DSS V2.0	
	AUP V5.0	
Describe the data output validation checks performed by the organization's application(s).	ISO/IEC 27001	A.12.2.4
	NIST SP 800-53	
	HIPAA Standard	
	PCI DSS V2.0	
	AUP V5.0	

Change Management

Describe the process for reviewing, prioritizing, and approving change requests, based on system and functionality.	ISO/IEC 27001	A.10.1.2
		A.12.5.1
	NIST SP 800-53	CM-3
	HIPAA Standard	
	PCI DSS V2.0	6.4
	AUP V5.0	G.21
Describe the test environments used for various systems to test changes prior to migration to the production environment.	ISO/IEC 27001	A.10.1.4
	NIST SP 800-53	
	HIPAA Standard	
	PCI DSS V2.0	6.4.1
	AUP V5.0	
Describe the testing process to include: • The types of data that shall be used in test environments (e.g., a copy of production data or simulated data) • Removal of test data and accounts before production systems become active	ISO/IEC 27001	A.10.1.4
		A.12.4.2
	NIST SP 800-53	
	HIPAA Standard	
	PCI DSS V2.0	6.4.3
		6.4.4
	AUP V5.0	
Describe the types of forms used in the change management process (e.g., change request forms) and the flow of change requests from request submission, approval, testing, testing approval, and implementation.	ISO/IEC 27001	A.12.4.1
	NIST SP 800-53	CM-3
	HIPAA Standard	
	PCI DSS V2.0	
	AUP V5.0	

continued

Change Management (continued)

Describe the procedures used to migrate changes securely to the production environment. For example, describe the controls in place to ensure that programmers cannot promote their own code.	ISO/IEC 27001	A.10.1.3
	NIST SP 800-53	CM-5
	HIPAA Standard	
	PCI DSS V2.0	6.4.2
	AUP V5.0	
Define the requirement to provide rollback procedures, including procedures and responsibilities for aborting and recovering from unsuccessful changes and unforeseen events.	ISO/IEC 27001	
	NIST SP 800-53	CM-3
	HIPAA Standard	
	PCI DSS V2.0	6.4.5.4
	AUP V5.0	
Describe the separation of the development/test environments and the production environment and the access controls in place to enforce the separation.	ISO/IEC 27001	A.10.1.3
		A.10.1.4
		A.12.4.3
	NIST SP 800-53	
	HIPAA Standard	
	PCI DSS V2.0	6.4.2
	AUP V5.0	
Describe the procedures for conducting postimplementation reviews after the implementation of significant changes.	ISO/IEC 27001	A.12.5.2
	NIST SP 800-53	SI-2
	HIPAA Standard	
	PCI DSS V2.0	
	AUP V5.0	
Describe the established procedures for defining, raising, assessing, and authorizing emergency changes that do not follow the established change control process.	ISO/IEC 27001	
	NIST SP 800-53	CM-3
	HIPAA Standard	
	PCI DSS V2.0	
	AUP V5.0	

Patch Management

Describe the procedures relating to security patch installation and patch management.	ISO/IEC 27001	A.12.5.1
	NIST SP 800-53	
	HIPAA Standard	
	PCI DSS V2.0	6.1
	AUP V5.0	
Describe processes used to identify newly discovered security vulnerabilities and to update the system configuration standards as new vulnerability issues are found.	ISO/IEC 27001	A.12.6.1
	NIST SP 800-53	RA-3
		SI-5
	HIPAA Standard	
	PCI DSS V2.0	6.2
	AUP V5.0	

Patch Management (continued)

Describe the procedure used for testing security patches before deployment into production.	ISO/IEC 27001	A.10.1.2
	NIST SP 800-53	CM-1
	HIPAA Standard	
	PCI DSS V2.0	6.4
	AUP V5.0	I.4

System Information Integrity and Monitoring

Firewall and Router Security Administration

Document the firewall and router configuration standards, incorporating the items below.	ISO/IEC 27001	A.10.1.2
	NIST SP 800-53	CM-1
	HIPAA Standard	
	PCI DSS V2.0	1.1
	AUP V5.0	
Describe the process for testing and approval of all network connections and changes to firewall and router configurations.	ISO/IEC 27001	A.10.6.1
	NIST SP 800-53	
	HIPAA Standard	
	PCI DSS V2.0	1.1.1
	AUP V5.0	
Define the groups, roles, and responsibilities for logical management of network components.	ISO/IEC 27001	
	NIST SP 800-53	
	HIPAA Standard	
	PCI DSS V2.0	1.1.4
	AUP V5.0	
Define the requirement that a current network diagram (e.g., one that shows sensitive or critical data flows over the network) must be maintained that shows connections to components storing or processing sensitive data, including any wireless networks.	ISO/IEC 27001	A.10.6.1
	NIST SP 800-53	
	HIPAA Standard	
	PCI DSS V2.0	1.1.2
	AUP V5.0	
Define the requirement that firewall configuration standards must exist that require a firewall at each Internet connection and between any DMZ (demilitarized zone—perimeter networking) and the internal network zone. NOTE: This must be defined in the firewall and router configuration standards.	ISO/IEC 27001	A.11.4.5
	NIST SP 800-53	AC-4
		SC-7
	HIPAA Standard	
	PCI DSS V2.0	1.1.3
	AUP V5.0	
Define and list the services, protocols, and ports necessary for business operations (e.g., hypertext transfer protocol [HTTP], secure sockets layer [SSL], secure shell [SSH] and virtual private network [VPN]). Document the business justification for each of the services used.	ISO/IEC 27001	
	NIST SP 800-53	
	HIPAA Standard	
	PCI DSS V2.0	1.1.5
	AUP V5.0	

continued

Firewall and Router Security Administration (continued)

Define the frequency of the review of firewall and router rule sets. NOTE: This must be defined in the firewall and router configuration standards.	ISO/IEC 27001		
	NIST SP 800-53		
	HIPAA Standard	164.308(a)(1)(ii)(D)	
	PCI DSS V2.0	1.1.6	
	AUP V5.0		
Describe how direct public access is prohibited between the Internet and any system component containing sensitive data. Restrictions may include: • Implement a DMZ to limit inbound traffic to only system components that provide authorized publicly accessible services, protocols, and ports. • Limit inbound Internet traffic to Internet protocol (IP) addresses within the DMZ. • Do not allow any direct connections inbound or outbound for traffic between the Internet and the cardholder data environment. • Do not allow internal addresses to pass from the Internet into the DMZ. • Do not allow unauthorized outbound traffic from the cardholder data environment to the Internet. • Implement stateful inspection, also known as dynamic packet filtering. • Place system components that store cardholder data (such as a database) in an internal network zone, segregated from the DMZ and other untrusted networks. Do not disclose private IP addresses and routing information to unauthorized parties. NOTE: Methods to obscure IP addressing may include, but are not limited to network address translation (NAT).	ISO/IEC 27001	A.11.4.5	
	NIST SP 800-53	AC-4	
		SC-7	
	HIPAA Standard		
	PCI DSS V2.0	1.3	
	AUP V5.0	G.17	
Define the requirement that personal firewall software must be installed on mobile and/or employee-owned computers with direct connectivity to the Internet (e.g., laptops used by employees) and that are used to access the organization's network. NOTE: This must be defined in the firewall and router configuration standards.	ISO/IEC 27001	A.11.4.6	
	NIST SP 800-53		
	HIPAA Standard		
	PCI DSS V2.0	1.4	
	AUP V5.0	G.17	

Network Security and Monitoring

Unless a flat network is used, describe how network segmentation, or isolating (segmenting), sensitive systems from the remainder of an entity's network is accomplished.	ISO/IEC 27001	A.11.4.5
	NIST SP 800-53	AC-4
	HIPAA Standard	
	PCI DSS V2.0	
	AUP V5.0	
Describe the controls in place to safeguard the confidentiality and integrity of sensitive data passing over public networks.	ISO/IEC 27001	A.10.6.1
	NIST SP 800-53	
	HIPAA Standard	164.312(e)(1)
	PCI DSS V2.0	4.1
	AUP V5.0	G.2
Describe the process for the review and deletion of inactive network and application user accounts.	ISO/IEC 27001	
	NIST SP 800-53	AC-2
	HIPAA Standard	
	PCI DSS V2.0	8.5.5
	AUP V5.0	H.4
Describe the process for management of vendor accounts used for support and maintenance of system components.	ISO/IEC 27001	A.10.6.2
	NIST SP 800-53	SA-9
	HIPAA Standard	
	PCI DSS V2.0	8.5.6
	AUP V5.0	
Describe the process implemented for the detection of unauthorized wireless devices.	ISO/IEC 27001	
	NIST SP 800-53	AC-18
	HIPAA Standard	
	PCI DSS V2.0	11.1
	AUP V5.0	
Describe the implementation of intrusion-detection systems and/or intrusion-prevention systems.	ISO/IEC 27001	
	NIST SP 800-53	
	HIPAA Standard	
	PCI DSS V2.0	10.6
		11.4
	AUP V5.0	G.1
		G.19
Describe the electronic mechanisms in place to detect the unauthorized alteration or destruction of sensitive information (e.g., file integrity software).	ISO/IEC 27001	
	NIST SP 800-53	SI-7
	HIPAA Standard	164.312(c)(2)
	PCI DSS V2.0	11.5
	AUP V5.0	

Audit Logging Controls

	Describe how audit logs are produced and kept for an agreed period of time to assist in future investigations and access-control monitoring.	ISO/IEC 27001	A.10.10.1
		NIST SP 800-53	AU-2
			AU-11
		HIPAA Standard	
		PCI DSS V2.0	10.1
			10.7
		AUP V5.0	G.4
			G.7
			G.9
	Describe the audit logging that is enabled for network components, servers, mainframes, midrange systems, and critical applications—especially those that process or store sensitive information (e.g., cardholder, personally identifiable information [PII], or protected health information [PHI]).	ISO/IEC 27001	A.10.10.1
		NIST SP 800-53	AU-2
			AU-3
		HIPAA Standard	164.312(b)
		PCI DSS V2.0	10.2
		AUP V5.0	G.4
			G.7
	Define the events that are logged, for example: • User ID • Type of event • Date and time • Success or failure indication • Origination of event • Identity or name of affected data, system component, or resource List all that apply. The above should be documented for each operating system and critical application.	ISO/IEC 27001	A.10.10.1
		NIST SP 800-53	AU-3
		HIPAA Standard	
		PCI DSS V2.0	10.3
		AUP V5.0	G.8
	Describe the procedures for audit log reviews and reporting discrepancies.	ISO/IEC 27001	A.10.10.2
		NIST SP 800-53	AU-6
		HIPAA Standard	164.308(a)(1)(ii)(D)
			164.308(a)(5)(ii)(C)
		PCI DSS V2.0	10.6
		AUP V5.0	G.4
	Define the frequency of audit log reviews.	ISO/IEC 27001	A.10.10.2
		NIST SP 800-53	AU-6
		HIPAA Standard	
		PCI DSS V2.0	10.6
		AUP V5.0	

Audit Logging Controls (continued)

If implemented, describe the use of centralized logging.	ISO/IEC 27001	A.10.10.3	
	NIST SP 800-53	AU-7	
	HIPAA Standard		
	PCI DSS V2.0	10.5.3	
	AUP V5.0		
Describe the controls in place to protect against log files being edited or deleted.	ISO/IEC 27001	A.10.10.3	
	NIST SP 800-53	AU-9	
	HIPAA Standard		
	PCI DSS V2.0	10.5	
	AUP V5.0		
Describe the use of time-synchronization technology (e.g., network time protocol [NTP]) that ensures that all critical system clocks are synchronized with an authoritative time source.	ISO/IEC 27001	A.10.10.6	
	NIST SP 800-53	AU-8	
	HIPAA Standard		
	PCI DSS V2.0	10.4	
	AUP V5.0		
Describe the use of file-integrity monitoring or change-detection software for audit logs.	ISO/IEC 27001		
	NIST SP 800-53	AU-9	
	HIPAA Standard		
	PCI DSS V2.0	10.5	
	AUP V5.0		

Antivirus and Mobile Code Protection

Define the requirement that antivirus technologies shall be deployed and the types of devices that must be protected by antivirus software.	ISO/IEC 27001	A.10.4.1	
	NIST SP 800-53	SI-3	
	HIPAA Standard	164.308(a)(5)(ii)(B)	
	PCI DSS V2.0	5.1	
	AUP V5.0	G.5	
		G.6	
Describe the type(s) of antivirus software in use and capabilities to detect, remove, and protect against all known types of malicious software.	ISO/IEC 27001	A.10.4.2	
	NIST SP 800-53	SI-3	
	HIPAA Standard		
	PCI DSS V2.0	5.1.1	
	AUP V5.0	G.5	
		G.6	
Define the requirement that the antivirus system must have a logging capability and that this feature is enabled.	ISO/IEC 27001	A.10.4	
	NIST SP 800-53		
	HIPAA Standard		
	PCI DSS V2.0	5.2	
	AUP V5.0		

Encryption

Define the requirement to mask sensitive data when displayed, according to regulatory requirements.	ISO/IEC 27001		
	NIST SP 800-53		
	HIPAA Standard		
	PCI DSS V2.0	3.3	
	AUP V5.0		
Describe how e-mails containing sensitive information are required to be encrypted. Describe how this is accomplished.	ISO/IEC 27001	A.10.8.4	
	NIST SP 800-53		
	HIPAA Standard		
	PCI DSS V2.0	4.2	
	AUP V5.0		
Document the policy or procedures that govern the use of cryptography across the organization. This may be included in the overall security policy document.	ISO/IEC 27001	A.12.3.1	
	NIST SP 800-53	SC-13	
	HIPAA Standard	164.308(a)(1)(ii)(B)	
	PCI DSS V2.0		
	AUP V5.0		
Describe how nonconsole administrative access to system components is encrypted. Include descriptions for all technologies such as SSH, VPN, or SSL/TLS (transport layer security).	ISO/IEC 27001		
	NIST SP 800-53		
	HIPAA Standard		
	PCI DSS V2.0	2.3	
	AUP V5.0	G.3	
		G.11	
		H.8	
Describe procedures for the management of cryptographic keys, including key distribution.	ISO/IEC 27001	A.12.3.2	
	NIST SP 800-53	SC-12	
	HIPAA Standard		
	PCI DSS V2.0	3.5	
		3.6	
	AUP V5.0		
Describe the cryptographic protections in use to encrypt and decrypt sensitive data or otherwise make it unreadable.	ISO/IEC 27001	A.12.3.1	
	NIST SP 800-53	SC-13	
	HIPAA Standard	164.312(a)(2)(iv)	
	PCI DSS V2.0	3.4	
	AUP V5.0		
Describe the relevant agreements, laws, and regulations considered when implementing the use of cryptography. Define what laws or regulations are applicable in the organization's environment.	ISO/IEC 27001	A.15.1.6	
	NIST SP 800-53	SC-13	
	HIPAA Standard		
	PCI DSS V2.0	3.4	
	AUP V5.0		

System Configuration and Hardening

Define the requirement and procedures that must be followed to configure newly installed network components securely.	ISO/IEC 27001	
	NIST SP 800-53	CM-6
	HIPAA Standard	
	PCI DSS V2.0	2.2
	AUP V5.0	I.3
Describe the techniques used for network hardening (e.g., limiting unnecessary protocols and services, etc.).	ISO/IEC 27001	
	NIST SP 800-53	
	HIPAA Standard	
	PCI DSS V2.0	2.2.2
	AUP V5.0	I.3

System Services Acquisition and Protection

Vendor and Third-Party Agreements

Describe the procedures that are followed, including a risk assessment that may be performed, before allowing an external party access to the organization's network or any application or database.	ISO/IEC 27001	A.6.2.1
	NIST SP 800-53	CA-3
	HIPAA Standard	
	PCI DSS V2.0	
	AUP V5.0	
Define the security requirements that must be fulfilled before granting a vendor or customer access to the organization's information or assets.	ISO/IEC 27001	A.6.2.2
	NIST SP 800-53	
	HIPAA Standard	164.308(b)(1)
	PCI DSS V2.0	
	AUP V5.0	P.2
Define the requirement that formal contracts shall be in place that contain all necessary security requirements to be followed by third parties.	ISO/IEC 27001	A.6.2.3
	NIST SP 800-53	CA-3
		PS-7
		SA-9
	HIPAA Standard	164.308(b)(4)
	PCI DSS V2.0	12.8
	AUP V5.0	C.2
Define and describe the use of a contract or memorandum of understanding (MOU), which must exist between the organization and the business associate, that requires the business associate to implement reasonable and appropriate administrative, physical, and technical safeguards to protect sensitive information.	ISO/IEC 27001	A.10.2.1
	NIST SP 800-53	
	HIPAA Standard	164.314(a)(2)(i)
		164.314(a)(2)(ii)
	PCI DSS V2.0	
	AUP V5.0	C.2
Describe how the security controls of third-party providers are periodically reviewed and verified.	ISO/IEC 27001	A.10.2.2
	NIST SP 800-53	SA-9
	HIPAA Standard	
	PCI DSS V2.0	
	AUP V5.0	P.3

System Interconnections

Document any existing exchange policy or procedure designed to protect the exchange of information with interconnected third parties.	ISO/IEC 27001	A.10.8.1	
	NIST SP 800-53	AC-20	
		CA-3	
		PS-6	
	HIPAA Standard		
	PCI DSS V2.0		
	AUP V5.0		
Define the requirement of an interconnection service agreement (ISA) or MOU for the exchange of information between the organization and external parties.	ISO/IEC 27001	A.10.8.2	
	NIST SP 800-53	CA-3	
		SA-9	
	HIPAA Standard		
	PCI DSS V2.0		
	AUP V5.0		
Describe the controls governing the appropriate use and security of electronic messaging.	ISO/IEC 27001	A.10.8.4	
	NIST SP 800-53		
	HIPAA Standard		
	PCI DSS V2.0	4.2	
	AUP V5.0		

Electronic Commerce

For systems involved in electronic commerce, describe how transactions passing over public networks are protected from fraudulent activity, contract dispute, and unauthorized disclosure and modification.	ISO/IEC 27001	A.10.9.1	
	NIST SP 800-53	SC-8	
		SC-9	
	HIPAA Standard		
	PCI DSS V2.0		
	AUP V5.0		
Describe the security controls in place to protect online transactions from incomplete transmission, misrouting, unauthorized message alteration, unauthorized disclosure, unauthorized message duplication, or replay.	ISO/IEC 27001	A.10.9.2	
	NIST SP 800-53		
	HIPAA Standard		
	PCI DSS V2.0		
	AUP V5.0		
Describe the controls in place to prevent the unauthorized modification of sensitive information being made available on a public network.	ISO/IEC 27001	A.10.9.3	
	NIST SP 800-53	SC-14	
	HIPAA Standard		
	PCI DSS V2.0		
	AUP V5.0		

Informational Asset Management

Media Handling

Describe the authorization required for media removal from the organization.	ISO/IEC 27001	A.10.7.1	
	NIST SP 800-53		
	HIPAA Standard	164.310(d)(1)	
	PCI DSS V2.0	9.8	
	AUP V5.0		
Define how media removals are recorded or logged and the documentation maintained.	ISO/IEC 27001	A.10.7.1	
	NIST SP 800-53	PE-16	
	HIPAA Standard	164.310(d)(1)	
	PCI DSS V2.0	9.8	
	AUP V5.0		
Describe the procedures to send media by secured courier or other delivery method that can be accurately tracked.	ISO/IEC 27001	A.10.8.3	
	NIST SP 800-53	MP-5	
	HIPAA Standard		
	PCI DSS V2.0	9.7.2	
	AUP V5.0		
Describe existing policies and procedures for the approval and documentation of media removal, including: • Tapes • Disks • USB drives • Tablets • Printed material	ISO/IEC 27001	A.10.7.1	
	NIST SP 800-53	MP-5	
	HIPAA Standard	164.310(d)(1)	
	PCI DSS V2.0	9.8	
	AUP V5.0	G.13	
Describe the controls in place to protect media that are transported between sites (reliable couriers, locked containers, etc.).	ISO/IEC 27001	A.10.7.3	
	NIST SP 800-53	MP-4	
	HIPAA Standard		
	PCI DSS V2.0	9.9	
	AUP V5.0	G.13	
Describe the formal procedures that securely and safely dispose of media that are no longer required.	ISO/IEC 27001	A.10.7.2	
	NIST SP 800-53	MP-6	
	HIPAA Standard	164.310(d)(2)(i)	
	PCI DSS V2.0	9.10.1	
	AUP V5.0		
Describe the procedures to sanitize information system media prior to release for reuse.	ISO/IEC 27001	A.10.7.2	
	NIST SP 800-53	MP-6	
	HIPAA Standard	164.310(d)(2)(ii)	
	PCI DSS V2.0	9.10.2	
	AUP V5.0		

Asset and Capacity Management

Describe how network and informational assets are identified and maintained in an IT asset inventory. Define the requirement that IT asset inventories must be performed at least annually.	ISO/IEC 27001	A.7.1.1
	NIST SP 800-53	CM-8
		PM-5
	HIPAA Standard	
	PCI DSS V2.0	9.9.1
	AUP V5.0	D.1
		P.1
Describe how informational assets identified in the IT asset inventory are associated with and owned by a specific individual or a designated part of the organization.	ISO/IEC 27001	A.7.1.2
	NIST SP 800-53	CM-8
	HIPAA Standard	
	PCI DSS V2.0	
	AUP V5.0	P.1
Describe the documenting system in place to manage all information systems' software licenses.	ISO/IEC 27001	
	NIST SP 800-53	SA-6
	HIPAA Standard	
	PCI DSS V2.0	
	AUP V5.0	
Describe how resources are monitored and tuned and projections made of future capacity requirements to ensure the availability and efficiency of systems.	ISO/IEC 27001	A.10.3.1
	NIST SP 800-53	
	HIPAA Standard	
	PCI DSS V2.0	
	AUP V5.0	

Continuity of Operations

Data Backup and Recovery

Describe the back-up and restoration procedures including the use of the following: • Logs or automatically generated alerts that document successful and failed backups • Secure off-site storage of backup media • Encryption employed during backups	ISO/IEC 27001	A.10.5.1
	NIST SP 800-53	CP-9
	HIPAA Standard	164.308(a)(7)(ii)(A)
	PCI DSS V2.0	9.5
	AUP V5.0	G.20
Describe procedures used to periodically restore data from backups to ensure the integrity of backup media.	ISO/IEC 27001	
	NIST SP 800-53	CP-10
	HIPAA Standard	164.308(a)(7)(ii)(B)
	PCI DSS V2.0	
	AUP V5.0	G.20

Data Backup and Recovery (continued)

Describe the process that maintains an inventory log of all backup media and requires that a media inventory be conducted at least annually.	ISO/IEC 27001	A.7.1.1
	NIST SP 800-53	CM-8
	HIPAA Standard	
	PCI DSS V2.0	9.9.1
	AUP V5.0	

Disaster Recovery (DR) and Business Continuity Planning (BCP)

Define the requirement that contingency plans must be developed and implemented to maintain or restore operations following an interruption or failure of critical business processes.	ISO/IEC 27001	A.14.1.1
	NIST SP 800-53	CP-1
		CP-2
	HIPAA Standard	164.308(a)(7)(i)
	PCI DSS V2.0	
	AUP V5.0	K.3
Define the requirement that a risk assessment, or business impact analysis (BIA) must be performed prior to the DR/BCP. Based on the results of the BIA, describe in the DR/BCP the events that can cause interruptions to business processes, along with the probability and impact of such interruptions and their consequences for information security.	ISO/IEC 27001	A.14.1.2
	NIST SP 800-53	CP-2
		RA-1
		RA-3
	HIPAA Standard	164.308(a)(7)(ii)(E)
	PCI DSS V2.0	
	AUP V5.0	K.1
		K.2
Define the frequency and describe the procedures for periodic testing and revision of contingency plans.	ISO/IEC 27001	A.14.1.5
	NIST SP 800-53	CP-4
	HIPAA Standard	164.308(a)(7)(ii)(D)
	PCI DSS V2.0	
	AUP V5.0	K.6

Incident Response Plan and Procedures

Describe the procedures for incident response.	ISO/IEC 27001	A.13.1.1
		A.13.1.2
		A.13.2.1
	NIST SP 800-53	IR-1
	HIPAA Standard	164.308(a)(6)(i)
	PCI DSS V2.0	12.9
	AUP V5.0	J.1
Describe procedures for periodically testing the incident response plan.	ISO/IEC 27001	A.13.2.2
	NIST SP 800-53	IR-3
	HIPAA Standard	
	PCI DSS V2.0	12.9.2
	AUP V5.0	

continued

Incident Response Plan and Procedures (continued)

	Describe the training that is provided to staff that are responsible for responding to security breaches.	ISO/IEC 27001	
		NIST SP 800-53	IR-2
		HIPAA Standard	
		PCI DSS V2.0	12.9.4
		AUP V5.0	
	Describe the procedures to respond to alerting from intrusion-detection, intrusion-prevention, and file-integrity monitoring systems, including detection of unauthorized wireless access points.	ISO/IEC 27001	
		NIST SP 800-53	AU-6
			CA-7
			IR-5
			IR-6
			SI-4
		HIPAA Standard	164.308(a)(1)(ii)(D)
		PCI DSS V2.0	12.9.5
		AUP V5.0	
	Describe how the organization identifies and responds to suspected or known security incidents and documents security incidents and their outcomes.	ISO/IEC 27001	A.13.2.1
		NIST SP 800-53	IR-4
			IR-6
			IR-8
		HIPAA Standard	164.308(a)(6)(ii)
		PCI DSS V2.0	12.5.3
		AUP V5.0	
	Describe the procedures that specify when and by whom authorities (e.g., law enforcement, fire department, supervisory authorities) should be contacted after an information security incident, if it is suspected that laws may have been broken.	ISO/IEC 27001	A.6.1.6
		NIST SP 800-53	IR-6
		HIPAA Standard	
		PCI DSS V2.0	
		AUP V5.0	
	Describe the procedures for collecting and presenting evidence for the purposes of disciplinary action.	ISO/IEC 27001	A.13.2.3
		NIST SP 800-53	IR-4
		HIPAA Standard	
		PCI DSS V2.0	
		AUP V5.0	
	Describe the process for modifying and evolving the incident response plan according to lessons learned and incorporating industry developments.	ISO/IEC 27001	A.13.2.2
		NIST SP 800-53	IR-4
		HIPAA Standard	
		PCI DSS V2.0	12.9.6
		AUP V5.0	

Appendix A: ISO/IEC 27001 (Annex A) Controls[(c) ISO]

(c) ISO This material is reproduced from ISO 27001:2005 with permission of the American National Standards Institute (ANSI) on behalf of the International Organization for Standardization (ISO). No part of this material may be copied or reproduced in any form, electronic retrieval system, or otherwise or made available on the Internet, a public network, by satellite or otherwise without the prior written consent of ANSI. Copies of this standard may be purchased from ANSI, 25 West 43rd Street, New York, NY 10036, (212) 642-4900, http://webstore.ansi.org

A.5 Security Policy

A.5.1 Information security policy

Objective: To provide management direction and support for information security in accordance with business requirements and relevant laws and regulations.

Management should set a clear policy direction in line with business objectives and demonstrate support for, and commitment to, information security through the issue and maintenance of an information security policy across the organization.

A.5.1.1 Information security policy document

Control: An information security policy document should be approved by management and published and communicated to all employees and relevant external parties.

A.5.1.2 Review of the information security policy

Control: The information security policy should be reviewed at planned intervals or if significant changes occur to ensure its continuing suitability, adequacy, and effectiveness.

A.6 Organization of Information Security

A.6.1 Internal

Objective: To manage information security within the organization. A management framework should be established to initiate and control the implementation of information security within the organization.

Management should approve the information security policy, assign security roles, and coordinate and review the implementation of security across the organization.

If necessary, a source of specialist information security advice should be established and made available within the organization. Contacts with external security specialists or groups, including relevant authorities, should be developed to keep up with industrial trends, monitor standards and assessment methods, and provide suitable liaison points when handling information security incidents. A multidisciplinary approach to information security should be encouraged.

A.6.1.1 Management commitment to information security
Control: Management should actively support security within the organization through clear direction, demonstrated commitment, explicit assignment, and acknowledgment of information security responsibilities.

A.6.1.2 Information security coordination
Control: Information security activities should be coordinated by representatives from different parts of the organization with relevant roles and job functions.

A.6.1.3 Allocation of information security responsibilities
Control: All information security responsibilities should be clearly defined.

A.6.1.4 Authorization process for information processing facilities
Control: A management authorization process for new information processing facilities should be defined and implemented.

A.6.1.5 Confidentiality agreements
Control: Requirements for confidentiality or nondisclosure agreements reflecting the organization's needs for the protection of information should be identified and regularly reviewed.

A.6.1.6 Contact with authorities
Control: Appropriate contacts with relevant authorities should be maintained.

A.6.1.7 Contact with special interest groups
Control: Appropriate contacts with special interest groups or other specialist security forums and professional associations should be maintained.

A.6.1.8 Independent review of information security

Control: The organization's approach to managing information security and its implementation (i.e., control objectives, controls, policies, processes, and procedures for information security) should be reviewed independently at planned intervals, or when significant changes to the security implementation occur.

A.6.2 External Parties

Objective: To maintain the security of the organization's information and information processing facilities that are accessed, processed, communicated to, or managed by external parties.

The security of the organization's information and information processing facilities should not be reduced by the introduction of external party products or services.

Any access to the organization's information processing facilities and processing and communication of information by external parties should be controlled.

Where there is a business need for working with external parties that may require access to the organization's information and information processing facilities, or in obtaining or providing a product and service from or to an external party, a risk assessment should be carried out to determine security implications and control requirements. Controls should be agreed and defined in an agreement with the external party.

A.6.2.1 Identification of risks related to external parties

Control: The risks to the organization's information and information processing facilities from business processes involving external parties should be identified and appropriate controls implemented before granting access.

A.6.2.2 Addressing security when dealing with customers

Control: All identified security requirements should be addressed before giving customers access to the organization's information or assets.

A.6.2.3 Addressing security in third-party agreements

Control: Agreements with third parties involving accessing, processing, communicating, or managing the organization's information or information processing facilities or adding products or services to information processing facilities should cover all relevant security requirements.

A.7 Asset Management
A.7.1 Responsibility for assets
Objective: To achieve and maintain appropriate protection of organizational assets.

All assets should be accounted for and have a nominated owner.

Owners should be identified for all assets and the responsibility for the maintenance of appropriate controls should be assigned. The implementation of specific controls may be delegated by the owner as appropriate but the owner remains responsible for the proper protection of the assets.

A.7.1.1 Inventory of assets
Control: All assets should be clearly identified and an inventory of all important assets drawn up and maintained.
A.7.1.2 Ownership of assets
Control: All information and assets associated with information processing facilities should be owned by a designated part of the organization.
A.7.1.3 Acceptable use of assets
Control: Rules for the acceptable use of information and assets associated with information processing facilities should be identified, documented, and implemented.

A.7.2 Information classification
Objective: To ensure that information receives an appropriate level of protection.

Information should be classified to indicate the need, priorities, and expected degree of protection when handling the information.

Information has varying degrees of sensitivity and criticality. Some items may require an additional level of protection or special handling. An information classification scheme should be used to define an appropriate set of protection levels and communicate the need for special handling measures.

A.7.2.1 Classification guidelines
Control: Information should be classified in terms of its value, legal requirements, sensitivity, and criticality to the organization.

A.7.2.2 Information labeling and handling
Control: An appropriate set of procedures for information labeling and handling should be developed and implemented in accordance with the classification scheme adopted by the organization.

A.8 Human Resources Security

A.8.1 Prior to employment
Objective: To ensure that employees, contractors, and third-party users understand their responsibilities and are suitable for the roles they are considered for, and to reduce the risk of theft, fraud, or misuse of facilities.

Security responsibilities should be addressed prior to employment in adequate job descriptions and in terms and conditions of employment.

All candidates for employment, contractors, and third-party users should be adequately screened, especially for sensitive jobs.

Employees, contractors, and third-party users of information processing facilities should sign an agreement on their security roles and responsibilities.

A.8.1.1 Roles and responsibilities
Control: Security roles and responsibilities of employees, contractors, and third-party users should be defined and documented in accordance with the organization's information security policy.

A.8.1.2 Screening
Control: Background verification checks on all candidates for employment, contractors, and third-party users should be carried out in accordance with relevant laws, regulations, and ethics and proportional to the business requirements, the classification of the information to be accessed, and the perceived risks.

A.8.1.3 Terms and conditions of employment

Control: As part of their contractual obligation, employees, contractors, and third-party users should agree and sign the terms and conditions of their employment contract, which should state their and the organization's responsibilities for information security.

A.8.2 During employment

Objective: To ensure that employees, contractors, and third-party users are aware of information security threats and concerns, their responsibilities and liabilities, and are equipped to support organizational security policy in the course of their normal work and to reduce the risk of human error.

Management responsibilities should be defined to ensure that security is applied throughout an individual's employment within the organization.

An adequate level of awareness, education, and training in security procedures and the correct use of information processing facilities should be provided to all employees, contractors, and third-party users to minimize possible security risks. A formal disciplinary process for handling security breaches should be established.

A.8.2.1 Management responsibilities

Control: Management should require employees, contractors, and third-party users to apply security in accordance with established policies and procedures of the organization.

A.8.2.2 Awareness, education, and training

Control: All employees of the organization and, where relevant, contractors and third party users should receive appropriate awareness training and regular updates in organizational policies and procedures, as relevant for their job function.

A.8.2.3 Disciplinary process

Control: There should be a formal disciplinary process for employees who have committed a security breach.

A.8.3 Termination or change of employment

Objective: To ensure that employees, contractors, and third-party users exit an organization or change employment in an orderly manner.

Responsibilities should be in place to ensure an employee's, contractor's, or third-party user's exit from the organization is managed, and that the return of all equipment and the removal of all access rights are completed.

Change of responsibilities and employments within an organization should be managed as the termination of the respective responsibility or employment in line with this section, and any new employments should be managed as described in Section 8.1.

A.8.3.1 Termination responsibilities

Control: Responsibilities for performing employment termination or change of employment should be clearly defined and assigned.

A.8.3.2 Return of assets

Control: All employees, contractors, and third-party users should return all of the organization's assets in their possession upon termination of their employment, contract, or agreement.

A.8.3.3 Removal of access rights

Control: The access rights of all employees, contractors, and third-party users to information and information processing facilities should be removed upon termination of their employment, contract, or agreement, or adjusted upon change.

A.9 Physical and Environmental Security
A.9.1 Secure areas

Objective: To prevent unauthorized physical access, damage, and interference to the organization's premises and information.

Critical or sensitive information processing facilities should be housed in secure areas, protected by defined security perimeters, with appropriate security barriers and entry controls. They should be physically protected from unauthorized access, damage, and interference.

The protection provided should be commensurate with the identified risks.

A.9.1.1 Physical security perimeter

Control: Security perimeters (barriers such as walls, card controlled entry gates, or manned reception desks) should be used to protect areas that contain information and information processing facilities.

A.9.1.2 Physical entry controls

Control: Secure areas should be protected by appropriate entry controls to ensure that only authorized personnel are allowed access.

A.9.1.3 Securing offices, rooms, facilities

Control: Physical security for offices, rooms, and facilities should be designed and applied.

A.9.1.4 Protecting against external and environmental threats

Control: Physical protection against damage from fire, flood, earthquake, explosion, civil unrest, and other forms of natural or man-made disaster should be designed and applied.

A.9.1.5 Working in secure areas

Control: Physical protection and guidelines for working in secure areas should be designed and applied.

A.9.1.6 Public access, delivery, and loading areas

Control: Access points such as delivery and loading areas and other points where unauthorized persons may enter the premises should be controlled and, if possible, isolated from information processing facilities to avoid unauthorized access.

A.9.2 Equipment security

Objective: To prevent loss, damage, theft, or compromise of assets and interruption to the organization's activities.

Equipment should be protected from physical and environmental threats.

Protection of equipment (including that used off-site, and the removal of property) is necessary to reduce the risk of unauthorized access to information and to protect against loss or damage. This should also consider equipment siting and disposal. Special controls may be required to protect against physical threats, and to safeguard supporting facilities, such as the electrical supply and cabling infrastructure.

A.9.2.1 Equipment siting and protection

Control: Equipment should be sited or protected to reduce the risks from environmental threats and hazards, and opportunities for unauthorized access.

A.9.2.2 Supporting utilities

Control: Equipment should be protected from power failures and other disruptions caused by failures in supporting utilities.

A.9.2.3 Cabling security

Control: Power and telecommunications cabling carrying data or supporting information services should be protected from interception or damage.

A.9.2.4 Equipment maintenance

Control: Equipment should be correctly maintained to ensure its continued availability and integrity.

A.9.2.5 Security of equipment off-premises

Control: Security should be applied to off-site equipment taking into account the different risks of working outside the organization's premises.

A.9.2.6 Secure disposal or reuse of equipment

Control: All items of equipment containing storage media should be checked to ensure that any sensitive data and licensed software have been removed or securely overwritten prior to disposal.

A.9.2.7 Removal of property

Control: Equipment, information, or software should not be taken off-site without prior authorization.

A.10 Communications and Operations Management

A.10.1 Operational procedures and responsibilities

Objective: To ensure the correct and secure operation of information processing facilities.

Responsibilities and procedures for the management and operation of all information processing facilities should be established. This includes the development of appropriate operating procedures.

Segregation of duties should be implemented, where appropriate, to reduce the risk of negligent or deliberate system misuse.

A.10.1.1 Documented operating procedures

Control: Operating procedures should be documented, maintained, and made available to all users who need them.

A.10.1.2 Change management

Control: Changes to information processing facilities and systems should be controlled.

A.10.1.3 Segregation of duties

Control: Duties and areas of responsibility should be segregated to reduce opportunities for unauthorized or unintentional modification or misuse of the organization's assets.

A.10.1.4 Separation of development, test, and operational facilities

Control: Development, test, and operational facilities should be separated to reduce the risks of unauthorized access or changes to the operational system.

A.10.2 Third-party service delivery management

Objective: To implement and maintain the appropriate level of information security and service delivery in line with third-party service delivery agreements.

The organization should check the implementation of agreements, monitor compliance with the agreements, and manage changes to ensure that the services delivered meet all requirements agreed with the third party.

A.10.2.1 Service delivery

Control: It should be ensured that the security controls, service definitions, and delivery levels included in the third-party service delivery agreement are implemented, operated, and maintained by the third party.

A.10.2.2 Monitoring and review of third-party services

Control: The services, reports, and records provided by the third party should be regularly monitored and reviewed, and audits should be carried out regularly.

A.10.2.3 Managing changes to third-party services

Control: Changes to the provision of services, including maintaining and improving existing information security policies, procedures, and controls, should be managed, taking account of the criticality of business systems and processes involved and reassessment of risks.

A.10.3 System planning and acceptance

Objective: To minimize the risk of system failures.

Advance planning and preparation are required to ensure the availability of adequate capacity and resources to deliver the required system performance.

Projections of future capacity requirements should be made to reduce the risk of system overload.

The operational requirements of new systems should be established, documented, and tested prior to their acceptance and use.

A.10.3.1 Capacity management

Control: The use of resources should be monitored, tuned, and projections made of future capacity requirements to ensure the required system performance.

A.10.3.2 System acceptance

Control: Acceptance criteria for new information systems, upgrades, and new versions should be established and suitable tests of the system(s) carried out during development and prior to acceptance.

A.10.4 Protection against malicious and mobile code

Objective: To protect the integrity of software and information.

Precautions are required to prevent and detect the introduction of malicious code and unauthorized mobile code.

Software and information processing facilities are vulnerable to the introduction of malicious code, such as computer viruses, network worms, Trojan horses, and logic bombs. Users should be made aware of the dangers of malicious code. Managers should, where appropriate, introduce controls to prevent, detect, and remove malicious code and control mobile code.

A.10.4.1 Controls against malicious code

Control: Detection, prevention, and recovery controls to protect against malicious code and appropriate user awareness procedures should be implemented.

A.10.4.2 Controls against mobile code

Control: Where the use of mobile code is authorized, the configuration should ensure that the authorized mobile code operates according to a clearly defined security policy, and unauthorized mobile code should be prevented from executing.

A.10.5 Backup

Objective: To maintain the integrity and availability of information and information processing facilities.

Routine procedures should be established to implement the agreed backup policy and strategy (see also 14.1) for taking backup copies of data and rehearsing their timely restoration.

A.10.5.1 Information backup

Control: Backup copies of information and software should be taken and tested regularly in accordance with the agreed backup policy.

A.10.6 Network security management

Objective: To ensure the protection of information in networks and the protection of the supporting infrastructure.

The secure management of networks, which may span organizational boundaries, requires careful consideration to data flow, legal implications, monitoring, and protection.

Additional controls may also be required to protect sensitive information passing over public networks.

A.10.6.1 Network controls

Control: Networks should be adequately managed and controlled, in order to be protected from threats and to maintain security for the systems and applications using the network, including information in transit.

A.10.6.2 Security of network services

Control: Security features, service levels, and management requirements of all network services should be identified and included in any network services agreement, whether these services are provided in-house or outsourced.

A.10.7 Media handling

Objective: To prevent unauthorized disclosure, modification, removal, or destruction of assets, and interruption to business activities.

Media should be controlled and physically protected.

Appropriate operating procedures should be established to protect documents, computer media (e.g., tapes, disks), input/output data, and system documentation from unauthorized disclosure, modification, removal, and destruction.

A.10.7.1 Management of removable media
Control: There should be procedures in place for the management of removable media.

A.10.7.2 Disposal of media
Control: Media should be disposed of securely and safely when no longer required, using formal procedures.

A.10.7.3 Information handling procedures
Control: Procedures for the handling and storage of information should be established to protect this information from unauthorized disclosure or misuse.

A.10.7.4 Security of system documentation
Control: System documentation should be protected against unauthorized access.

A.10.8 Exchange of information
Objective: To maintain the security of information and software exchanged within an organization and with any external entity.

Exchanges of information and software between organizations should be based on a formal exchange policy, carried out in line with exchange agreements, and should be compliant with any relevant legislation (see clause 15).

Procedures and standards should be established to protect information and physical media containing information in transit.

A.10.8.1 Information exchange policies and procedures
Control: Formal exchange policies, procedures, and controls should be in place to protect the exchange of information through the use of all types of communication facilities.

A.10.8.2 Exchange agreements
Control: Agreements should be established for the exchange of information and software between the organization and external parties.

A.10.8.3 Physical media in transit

Control: Media containing information should be protected against unauthorized access, misuse, or corruption during transportation beyond an organization's physical boundaries.

A.10.8.4 Electronic messaging

Control: Information involved in electronic messaging should be appropriately protected.

A.10.8.5 Business information systems

Control: Policies and procedures should be developed and implemented to protect information associated with the interconnection of business information systems.

A.10.9 Electronic commerce services

Objective: To ensure the security of electronic commerce services and their secure use.

The security implications associated with using electronic commerce services, including online transactions, and the requirements for controls should be considered. The integrity and availability of information electronically published through publicly available systems should also be considered.

A.10.9.1 Electronic commerce

Control: Information involved in electronic commerce passing over public networks should be protected from fraudulent activity, contract dispute, and unauthorized disclosure and modification.

A.10.9.2 Online transactions

Control: Information involved in online transactions should be protected to prevent incomplete transmission, misrouting, unauthorized message alteration, unauthorized disclosure, unauthorized message duplication, or replay.

A.10.9.3 Publicly available information

Control: The integrity of information being made available on a publicly available system should be protected to prevent unauthorized modification.

A.10.10 Monitoring

Objective: To detect unauthorized information processing activities.

Systems should be monitored and information security events should be recorded. Operator logs and fault logging should be used to ensure information system problems are identified.

An organization should comply with all relevant legal requirements applicable to its monitoring and logging activities.

System monitoring should be used to check the effectiveness of controls adopted and to verify conformity to an access policy model.

A.10.10.1 Audit logging
Control: Audit logs recording user activities, exceptions, and information security events should be produced and kept for an agreed period to assist in future investigations and access control monitoring.

A.10.10.2 Monitoring system use
Control: Procedures for monitoring use of information processing facilities should be established and the results of the monitoring activities reviewed regularly.

A.10.10.3 Protection of log information
Control: Logging facilities and log information should be protected against tampering and unauthorized access.

A.10.10.4 Administrator and operator logs
Control: System administrator and system operator activities should be logged.

A.10.10.5 Fault logging
Control: Faults should be logged, analyzed, and appropriate action taken.

A.10.10.6 Clock synchronization
Control: The clocks of all relevant information processing systems within an organization or security domain should be synchronized with an agreed accurate time source.

A.11 Access Control
A.11.1 Business requirement for access control
Objective: To control access to information.

Access to information, information processing facilities, and business processes should be controlled on the basis of business and security requirements.

Access control rules should take account of policies for information dissemination and authorization.

A.11.1.1 Access control policy

Control: An access control policy should be established, documented, and reviewed based on business and security requirements for access.

A.11.2 User access management

Objective: To ensure authorized user access and to prevent unauthorized access to information systems.

Formal procedures should be in place to control the allocation of access rights to information systems and services.

The procedures should cover all stages in the life cycle of user access, from the initial registration of new users to the final deregistration of users who no longer require access to information systems and services. Special attention should be given, where appropriate, to the need to control the allocation of privileged access rights, which allow users to override system controls.

A.11.2.1 User registration

Control: There should be a formal user registration and deregistration procedure in place for granting and revoking access to all information systems and services.

A.11.2.2 Privilege management

Control: The allocation and use of privileges should be restricted and controlled.

A.11.2.3 User password management

Control: The allocation of passwords should be controlled through a formal management process.

A.11.2.4 Review of user access rights

Control: Management should review users' access rights at regular intervals using a formal process.

A.11.3 User responsibilities

Objective: To prevent unauthorized user access, and compromise or theft of information and information processing facilities.

The cooperation of authorized users is essential for effective security.

Users should be made aware of their responsibilities for maintaining effective access controls, particularly regarding the use of passwords and the security of user equipment.

A clear desk and clear screen policy should be implemented to reduce the risk of unauthorized access or damage to papers, media, and information processing facilities.

A.11.3.1 Password use
Control: Users should be required to follow good security practices in the selection and use of passwords.

A.11.3.2 Unattended user equipment
Control: Users should ensure that unattended equipment has appropriate protection.

A.11.3.3 Clear desk and clear screen policy
Control: A clear desk policy for papers and removable storage media and a clear screen policy for information processing facilities shall be adopted.

A.11.4 Network access control
Objective: To prevent unauthorized access to networked services.

Access to both internal and external networked services should be controlled.

User access to networks and network services should not compromise the security of the network services by ensuring:

a. appropriate interfaces are in place between the organization's network and networks owned by other organizations, and public networks;
b. appropriate authentication mechanisms are applied for users and equipment; and
c. control of user access to information services is enforced.

A.11.4.1 Policy on use of network services
Control: Users should only be provided with access to the services that they have been specifically authorized to use.

A.11.4.2 User authentication for external connections
Control: Appropriate authentication methods should be used to control access by remote users.

A.11.4.3 Equipment identification in networks

Control: Automatic equipment identification should be considered as a means to authenticate connections from specific locations and equipment.

A.11.4.4 Remote diagnostic and configuration port protection

Control: Physical and logical access to diagnostic and configuration ports should be controlled.

A.11.4.5 Segregation in networks

Control: Groups of information services, users, and information systems should be segregated on networks.

A.11.4.6 Network connection control

Control: For shared networks, especially those extending across the organization's boundaries, the capability of users to connect to the network should be restricted, in line with the access control policy and requirements of the business applications (see 11.1).

A.11.4.7 Network routing control

Control: Routing controls should be implemented for networks to ensure that computer connections and information flows do not breach the access control policy of the business applications.

A.11.5 Operating system access control

Objective: To prevent unauthorized access to operating systems.

Security facilities should be used to restrict access to operating systems to authorized users. The facilities should be capable of the following:

a. authenticating authorized users, in accordance with a defined access control policy;
b. recording successful and failed system authentication attempts;
c. recording the use of special system privileges;
d. issuing alarms when system security policies are breached;
e. providing appropriate means for authentication;
f. where appropriate, restricting the connection time of users.

A.11.5.1 Secure log-on procedures

Control: Access to operating systems should be controlled by a secure log-on procedure.

A.11.5.2 User identification and authentication

Control: All users should have a unique identifier (user ID) for their personal use only, and a suitable authentication technique should be chosen to substantiate the claimed identity of a user.

A.11.5.3 Password management system

Control: Systems for managing passwords should be interactive and should ensure quality passwords.

A.11.5.4 Use of system utilities

Control: The use of utility programs that might be capable of overriding system and application controls should be restricted and tightly controlled.

A.11.5.5 Session time-out

Control: Inactive sessions should shut down after a defined period of inactivity.

A.11.5.6 Limitation of connection time

Control: Restrictions on connection times should be used to provide additional security for high-risk applications.

A.11.6 Application and information access control

Objective: To prevent unauthorized access to information held in application systems.

Security facilities should be used to restrict access to and within application systems.

Logical access to application software and information should be restricted to authorized users. Application systems should:

a. control user access to information and application system functions, in accordance with a defined access control policy;
b. provide protection from unauthorized access by any utility, operating system software, and malicious software that are capable of overriding or bypassing system or application controls;
c. not compromise other systems with which information resources are shared.

A.11.6.1 Information access restriction

Control: Access to information and application system functions by users and support personnel should be restricted in accordance with the defined access control policy.

A.11.6.2 Sensitive system isolation

Control: Sensitive systems should have a dedicated (isolated) computing environment.

A.11.7 Mobile computing and teleworking

Objective: To ensure information security when using mobile computing and teleworking facilities.

The protection required should be commensurate with the risks these specific ways of working cause.

When using mobile computing, the risks of working in an unprotected environment should be considered and appropriate protection applied. In the case of teleworking, the organization should apply protection to the teleworking site and ensure that suitable arrangements are in place for this way of working.

A.11.7.1 Mobile computing and communications

Control: A formal policy should be in place, and appropriate security measures should be adopted to protect against the risks of using mobile computing and communication facilities.

A.11.7.2 Teleworking

Objective: A policy, operational plans, and procedures should be developed and implemented for teleworking activities.

A.12 Information Systems Acquisition, Development, and Maintenance

A.12.1 Security requirements of information systems

Objective: To ensure that security is an integral part of information systems.

Information systems include operating systems, infrastructure, business applications, off-the-shelf products, services, and user-developed applications. The design and implementation of the information system supporting the business process can be crucial for security. Security requirements should be identified and agreed prior to the development and/or implementation of information systems.

All security requirements should be identified at the requirements phase of a project and justified, agreed, and documented as part of the overall business case for an information system.

A.12.1.1 Security requirements analysis and specification
Control: Statements of business requirements for new information systems or enhancements to existing information systems shall specify the requirements for security controls.

A.12.2 Correct processing in applications
Objective: To prevent errors, loss, unauthorized modification, or misuse of information in applications.

Appropriate controls should be designed into applications, including user-developed applications, to ensure correct processing. These controls should include the validation of input data, internal processing, and output data.

Additional controls may be required for systems that process, or have an impact on, sensitive, valuable, or critical information. Such controls should be determined on the basis of security requirements and risk assessment.

A.12.2.1 Input data validation
Control: Data input to applications should be validated to ensure that these data are correct and appropriate.

A.12.2.2 Control of internal processing
Control: Validation checks should be incorporated into applications to detect any corruption of information through processing errors or deliberate acts.

A.12.2.3 Message integrity
Control: Requirements for ensuring authenticity and protecting message integrity in applications should be identified, and appropriate controls identified and implemented.

A.12.2.4 Output data validation
Control: Data output from an application should be validated to ensure that the processing of stored information is correct and appropriate to the circumstances.

A.12.3 Cryptographic controls
Objective: To protect the confidentiality, authenticity, or integrity of information by cryptographic means.

A policy should be developed on the use of cryptographic controls. Key management should be in place to support the use of cryptographic techniques.

A.12.3.1 Policy on the use of cryptographic controls

Control: A policy on the use of cryptographic controls for protection of information should be developed and implemented.

A.12.3.2 Key management

Control: Key management should be in place to support the organization's use of cryptographic techniques.

A.12.4 Security of system files

Objective: To ensure the security of system files.

Access to system files and program source code should be controlled, and IT projects and support activities conducted in a secure manner. Care should be taken to avoid exposure of sensitive data in test environments.

A.12.4.1 Control of operational software

Control: There should be procedures in place to control the installation of software on operational systems.

A.12.4.2 Protection of system test data

Control: Test data should be selected carefully, and protected and controlled.

A.12.4.3 Access control to program source code

Control: Access to program source code should be restricted.

A.12.5 Security in development and support processes

Objective: To maintain the security of application system software and information.

Project and support environments should be strictly controlled.

Managers responsible for application systems should also be responsible for the security of the project or support environment. They should ensure that all proposed system changes are reviewed to check that they do not compromise the security of either the system or the operating environment.

A.12.5.1 Change control procedures

Control: The implementation of changes should be controlled by the use of formal change control procedures.

A.12.5.2 Technical review of applications after operating system changes

Control: When operating systems are changed, business critical applications should be reviewed and tested to ensure there is no adverse impact on organizational operations or security.

A.12.5.3 Restrictions on changes to software packages

Control: Modifications to software packages should be discouraged, limited to necessary changes, and all changes should be strictly controlled.

A.12.5.4 Information leakage

Control: Opportunities for information leakage should be prevented.

A.12.5.5 Outsourced software development

Control: Outsourced software development should be supervised and monitored by the organization.

A.12.6 Technical vulnerability management

Objective: To reduce risks resulting from exploitation of published technical vulnerabilities.

Technical vulnerability management should be implemented in an effective, systematic, and repeatable way with measurements taken to confirm its effectiveness. These considerations should include operating systems and any other applications in use.

A.12.6.1 Control of technical vulnerabilities

Control: Timely information about technical vulnerabilities of information systems being used should be obtained, the organization's exposure to such vulnerabilities evaluated, and appropriate measures taken to address the associated risk.

A.13 Information Security Incident Management
A.13.1 Reporting information security events and weaknesses

Objective: To ensure information security events and weaknesses associated with information systems are communicated in a manner allowing timely corrective action to be taken.

Formal event reporting and escalation procedures should be in place. All employees, contractors, and third-party users should be made aware of the procedures for reporting the different types of event and weakness that might have an impact on the security of organizational assets. They should be required to report any information security events and weaknesses as quickly as possible to the designated point of contact.

A.13.1.1 Reporting information security events

Control: Information security events should be reported through appropriate management channels as quickly as possible.

A.13.1.2 Reporting security weaknesses

Control: All employees, contractors, and third-party users of information systems and services should be required to note and report any observed or suspected security weaknesses in systems or services.

A.13.2 Management of information security incidents and improvements

Objective: To ensure a consistent and effective approach is applied to the management of information security incidents.

Responsibilities and procedures should be in place to handle information security events and weaknesses effectively once they have been reported. A process of continual improvement should be applied to the response to, monitoring, evaluating, and overall management of information security incidents.

Where evidence is required, it should be collected to ensure compliance with legal requirements.

A.13.2.1 Responsibilities and procedures

Control: Management responsibilities and procedures should be established to ensure a quick, effective, and orderly response to information security incidents.

A.13.2.2 Learning from information security incidents

Control: There should be mechanisms in place to enable the types, volumes, and costs of information security incidents to be quantified and monitored.

A.13.2.3 Collection of evidence

Control: Where a follow-up action against a person or organization after an information security incident involves legal action (either civil or criminal), evidence should be collected, retained, and presented to conform to the rules for evidence laid down in the relevant jurisdiction(s).

A.14 Business Continuity Management
A.14.1 Information security aspects of business continuity management

Objective: To counteract interruptions to business activities and to protect critical business processes from the effects of major failures of information systems or disasters and to ensure their timely resumption.

A business continuity management process should be implemented to minimize the impact on the organization and recover from loss of information assets (which may be the result of, for example, natural disasters, accidents, equipment failures, and deliberate actions) to an acceptable level through a combination of preventive and recovery controls. This process should identify the critical business processes and integrate the information security management requirements of business continuity with other continuity requirements relating to such aspects as operations, staffing, materials, transport, and facilities.

The consequences of disasters, security failures, loss of service, and service availability should be subject to a business impact analysis. Business continuity plans should be developed and implemented to ensure timely resumption of essential operations. Information security should be an integral part of the overall business continuity process, and other management processes within the organization.

Business continuity management should include controls to identify and reduce risks, in addition to the general risks assessment process, limit the consequences of damaging incidents, and ensure that information required for business processes is readily available.

A.14.1.1 Including information security in the business continuity management process

Control: A managed process should be developed and maintained for business continuity throughout the organization that addresses the information security requirements needed for the organization's business continuity.

A.14.1.2 Business continuity and risk assessment

Control: Events that can cause interruptions to business processes should be identified, along with the probability and impact of such interruptions and their consequences for information security.

A.14.1.3 Developing and implementing continuity plans including information security

Control: Plans should be developed and implemented to maintain or restore operations and ensure availability of information at the required level and in the required time scales following interruption to, or failure of, critical business processes.

A.14.1.4 Business continuity planning framework

Control: A single framework of business continuity plans should be maintained to ensure all plans are consistent, to consistently address information security requirements, and to identify priorities for testing and maintenance.

A.14.1.5 Testing, maintaining, and reassessing business continuity plans

Control: Business continuity plans should be tested and updated regularly to ensure that they are up to date and effective.

A.15 Compliance

A.15.1 Compliance with legal requirements

Objective: To avoid breaches of any law, statutory, regulatory, or contractual obligations, and of any security requirements.

The design, operation, use, and management of information systems may be subject to statutory, regulatory, and contractual security requirements.

Advice on specific legal requirements should be sought from the organization's legal advisers, or suitably qualified legal practitioners. Legislative requirements vary from country to country and may vary for information created in one country that is transmitted to another country (i.e., trans-border data flow).

A.15.1.1 Identification of applicable legislation

Control: All relevant statutory, regulatory, and contractual requirements and the organization's approach to meet these requirements should be explicitly defined, documented, and kept up to date for each information system and the organization.

A.15.1.2 Intellectual property rights (IPR)

Control: Appropriate procedures should be implemented to ensure compliance with legislative, regulatory, and contractual requirements on the use of material in respect of which there may be intellectual property rights and on the use of proprietary software products.

A.15.1.3 Protection of organizational records

Control: Important records should be protected from loss, destruction, and falsification, in accordance with statutory, regulatory, contractual, and business requirements.

A.15.1.4 Data protection and privacy of personal information

Control: Data protection and privacy should be ensured as required in relevant legislation, regulations, and, if applicable, contractual clauses.

A.15.1.5 Prevention of misuse of information processing facilities

Control: Users should be deterred from using information processing facilities for unauthorized purposes.

A.15.1.6 Regulation of cryptographic controls

Control: Cryptographic controls should be used in compliance with all relevant agreements, laws, and regulations.

A.15.2 Compliance with security policies and standards, and technical compliance

Objective: To ensure compliance of systems with organizational security policies and standards.

The security of information systems should be regularly reviewed.

Such reviews should be performed against the appropriate security policies and the technical platforms and information systems should be audited for compliance with applicable security implementation standards and documented security controls.

A.15.2.1 Compliance with security policies and standards

Control: Managers should ensure that all security procedures within their area of responsibility are carried out correctly to achieve compliance with security policies and standards.

A.15.2.2 Technical compliance checking

Control: Information systems should be regularly checked for compliance with security implementation standards.

A.15.3 Information systems audit considerations

Objective: To maximize the effectiveness of and to minimize interference to/from the information systems audit process.

There should be controls to safeguard operational systems and audit tools during information systems audits.

Protection is also required to safeguard the integrity and prevent misuse of audit tools.

A.15.3.1 Information systems audit controls

Control: Audit requirements and activities involving checks on operational systems should be carefully planned and agreed to minimize the risk of disruptions to business processes.

A.15.3.2 Protection of information systems audit tools

Control: Access to information systems audit tools should be protected to prevent any possible misuse or compromise.

Appendix B: NIST SP 800-53 Controls

FAMILY: ACCESS CONTROL
CLASS: TECHNICAL

AC-1 ACCESS CONTROL POLICY AND PROCEDURES
Control: The organization develops, disseminates, and reviews/updates [*Assignment: organization-defined frequency*]:

a. A formal, documented access ___ rol policy that addresses purpose, scope, roles ___, management commitment, coordin ___ nal entities, and compliance; and

b. Formal, docum ___ ate the implementation of the access ___ ted access controls.

AC-2 ACCOUNT M ___
Control: The organizati ___ ation system accounts, including:

a. Identifying account types (i.e., individual, group, system, application, guest/anonymous, and temporary);
b. Establishing conditions for group membership;
c. Identifying authorized users of the information system and specifying access privileges;
d. Requiring appropriate approvals for requests to establish accounts;
e. Establishing, activating, modifying, disabling, and removing accounts;
f. Specifically authorizing and monitoring the use of guest/anonymous and temporary accounts;
g. Notifying account managers when temporary accounts are no longer required and when information system users are terminated, transferred, or information system usage or need-to-know/need-to-share changes;
h. Deactivating: (i) temporary accounts that are no longer required; and (ii) accounts of terminated or transferred users;
i. Granting access to the system based on: (i) a valid access authorization; (ii) intended system usage; and (iii) other attributes as required by the organization or associated missions/business functions; and

j. Reviewing accounts [Assignment: organization-defined frequency].

AC-3 ACCESS ENFORCEMENT

Control: The information system enforces approved authorizations for logical access to the system in accordance with applicable policy.

AC-4 INFORMATION FLOW ENFORCEMENT

Control: The information system enforces approved authorizations for controlling the flow of information within the system and between interconnected systems in accordance with applicable policy.

AC-5 SEPARATION OF DUTIES

Control: The organization:

a. Separates duties of individuals as necessary, to prevent malevolent activity without collusion;
b. Documents separation of duties; and
c. Implements separation of duties through assigned information system access authorizations.

AC-6 LEAST PRIVILEGE

Control: The organization employs the concept of least privilege, allowing only authorized accesses for users (and processes acting on behalf of users) which are necessary to accomplish assigned tasks in accordance with organizational missions and business functions.

AC-7 UNSUCCESSFUL LOG-IN ATTEMPTS

Control: The information system:

a. Enforces a limit of [Assignment: organization-defined number] consecutive invalid log-in attempts by a user during a [Assignment: organization-defined time period]; and
b. Automatically [Selection: locks the account/node for an [Assignment: organization-defined time period]; locks the account/node until released by an administrator; delays next log-in prompt according to [Assignment: organization-defined delay algorithm]] when the maximum number of unsuccessful attempts is exceeded. The control applies regardless of whether the log-in occurs via a local or network connection.

AC-8 SYSTEM USE NOTIFICATION

Control: The information system:

a. Displays an approved system use notification message or banner before granting access to the system that provides privacy and security notices consistent with applicable federal laws, Executive Orders, directives, policies, regulations, standards, and guidance and states that: (i) users are accessing a US Government information system; (ii) system usage may be monitored, recorded, and subject to audit; (iii) unauthorized use of the system is prohibited and subject to criminal and civil penalties; and (iv) use of the system indicates consent to monitoring and recording;

b. Retains the notification message or banner on the screen until users take explicit actions to log on to or further access the information system; and

c. For publicly accessible systems: (i) displays the system use information when appropriate, before granting further access; (ii) displays references, if any, to monitoring, recording, or auditing that are consistent with privacy accommodations for such systems that generally prohibit those activities; and (iii) includes in the notice given to public users of the information system, a description of the authorized uses of the system.

AC-9 PREVIOUS LOG-ON (ACCESS) NOTIFICATION

Control: The information system notifies the user, upon successful log-on (access), of the date and time of the last log-on (access).

AC-10 CONCURRENT SESSION CONTROL

Control: The information system limits the number of concurrent sessions for each system account to [Assignment: organization-defined number].

AC-11 SESSION LOCK

Control: The information system:

a. Prevents further access to the system by initiating a session lock after [Assignment: organization-defined time period] of inactivity or upon receiving a request from a user; and

b. Retains the session lock until the user reestablishes access using established identification and authentication procedures.

AC-12 SESSION TERMINATION
[Withdrawn: Incorporated into SC-10]

AC-13 SUPERVISION AND REVIEW-ACCESS CONTROL
[Withdrawn: Incorporated into AC-2 and AU-6]

AC-14 PERMITTED ACTIONS WITHOUT IDENTIFICATION OR AUTHENTICATION
Control: The organization:

a. Identifies specific user actions that can be performed on the information system without identification or authentication; and
b. Documents and provides supporting rationale in the security plan for the information system, user actions not requiring identification, and authentication.

AC-15 AUTOMATED MARKING
[Withdrawn: Incorporated into MP-3]

AC-16 SECURITY ATTRIBUTES
Control: The information system supports and maintains the binding of [Assignment: organization-defined security attributes] to information in storage, in process, and in transmission.

AC-17 REMOTE ACCESS
Control: The organization:

a. Documents allowed methods of remote access to the information system;
b. Establishes usage restrictions and implementation guidance for each allowed remote access method;
c. Monitors for unauthorized remote access to the information system;
d. Authorizes remote access to the information system prior to connection; and
e. Enforces requirements for remote connections to the information system.

AC-18 WIRELESS ACCESS
Control: The organization:

a. Establishes usage restrictions and implementation guidance for wireless access;

b. Monitors for unauthorized wireless access to the information system;

c. Authorizes wireless access to the information system prior to connection; and

d. Enforces requirements for wireless connections to the information system.

AC-19 ACCESS CONTROL FOR MOBILE DEVICES

Control: The organization:

a. Establishes usage restrictions and implementation guidance for organization-controlled mobile devices;

b. Authorizes connection of mobile devices meeting organizational usage restrictions and implementation guidance to organizational information systems and Special Publication 800-53 Recommended Security Controls for Federal Information Systems and Organizations;

c. Monitors for unauthorized connections of mobile devices to organizational information systems;

d. Enforces requirements for the connection of mobile devices to organizational information systems;

e. Disables information system functionality that provides the capability for automatic execution of code on mobile devices without user direction;

f. Issues specially configured mobile devices to individuals traveling to locations that the organization deems to be of significant risk in accordance with organizational policies and procedures; and

g. Applies [Assignment: organization-defined inspection and preventative measures] to mobile devices returning from locations that the organization deems to be of significant risk in accordance with organizational policies and procedures.

AC-20 USE OF EXTERNAL INFORMATION SYSTEMS

Control: The organization establishes terms and conditions consistent with any trust relationships established with other organizations owning, operating, and/or maintaining external information systems, allowing authorized individuals to:

a. Access the information system from the external information systems; and

b. Process, store, and/or transmit organization-controlled information using the external information systems.

AC-21 USER-BASED COLLABORATION AND INFORMATION SHARING

Control: The organization:

a. Facilitates information sharing by enabling authorized users to determine whether access authorizations assigned to the sharing partner match the access restrictions on the information for [Assignment: organization-defined information sharing circumstances where user discretion is required]; and

b. Employs [Assignment: list of organization-defined information sharing circumstances and automated mechanisms or manual processes required] to assist users in making information sharing/collaboration decisions.

AC-22 PUBLICLY ACCESSIBLE CONTENT

Control: The organization:

a. Designates individuals authorized to post information onto an organizational information system that is publicly accessible;

b. Trains authorized individuals to ensure that publicly accessible information does not contain nonpublic information;

c. Reviews the proposed content of publicly accessible information for nonpublic information prior to posting onto the organizational information system;

d. Reviews the content on the publicly accessible organizational information system for nonpublic information [Assignment: organization-defined frequency]; and

e. Removes nonpublic information from the publicly accessible organizational information system, if discovered.

FAMILY: AWARENESS AND TRAINING
CLASS: OPERATIONAL

AT-1 SECURITY AWARENESS AND TRAINING POLICY AND PROCEDURES

Control: The organization develops, disseminates, and reviews/updates [Assignment: organization-defined frequency]:

a. A formal, documented security awareness and training policy that addresses purpose, scope, roles, responsibilities, management commitment, coordination among organizational entities, and compliance; and

b. Formal, documented procedures to facilitate the implementation of the security awareness and training policy and associated security awareness and training controls.

AT-2 SECURITY AWARENESS

Control: The organization provides basic security awareness training to all information system users (including managers, senior executives, and contractors) as part of initial training for new users, when required by system changes, and [Assignment: organization-defined frequency] thereafter.

AT-3 SECURITY TRAINING

Control: The organization provides role-based security-related training: (i) before authorizing access to the system or performing assigned duties; (ii) when required by system changes; and (iii) [Assignment: organization-defined frequency] thereafter.

AT-4 SECURITY TRAINING RECORDS

Control: The organization:

a. Documents and monitors individual information system security training activities, including basic security awareness training and specific information system security training; and

b. Retains individual training records for [Assignment: organization-defined time period].

AT-5 CONTACTS WITH SECURITY GROUPS AND ASSOCIATIONS

Control: The organization establishes and institutionalizes contact with selected groups and associations within the security community:

- To facilitate ongoing security education and training for organizational personnel;
- To stay up to date with the latest recommended security practices, techniques, and technologies; and
- To share current security-related information including threats, vulnerabilities, and incidents.

FAMILY: AUDIT AND ACCOUNTABILITY
CLASS: TECHNICAL

AU-1 AUDIT AND ACCOUNTABILITY POLICY AND PROCEDURES

Control: The organization develops, disseminates, and reviews/updates [Assignment: organization-defined frequency]:

    a. A formal, documented audit and accountability policy that addresses purpose, scope, roles, responsibilities, management commitment, coordination among organizational entities, and compliance; and

    b. Formal, documented procedures to facilitate the implementation of the audit and accountability policy and associated audit and accountability controls.

AU-2 AUDITABLE EVENTS

Control: The organization:

    a. Determines, based on a risk assessment and mission/business needs, that the information system must be capable of auditing the following events: [Assignment: organization-defined list of auditable events];

    b. Coordinates the security audit function with other organizational entities requiring audit-related information to enhance mutual support and to help guide the selection of auditable events;

    c. Provides a rationale for why the list of auditable events is deemed to be adequate to support after-the-fact investigations of security incidents; and

    d. Determines, based on current threat information and ongoing assessment of risk, that the following events are to be audited within the information system: [Assignment: organization-defined subset of the auditable events defined in AU-2a to be audited along with the frequency of (or situation requiring) auditing for each identified event].

AU-3 CONTENT OF AUDIT RECORDS

Control: The information system produces audit records that contain sufficient information to, at a minimum, establish what type of event occurred, when (date and time) the event occurred, where the event occurred, the source of the event, the outcome (success or failure) of the event, and the identity of any user/subject associated with the event.

AU-4 AUDIT STORAGE CAPACITY

Control: The organization allocates audit record storage capacity and configures auditing to reduce the likelihood of such capacity being exceeded.

AU-5 RESPONSE TO AUDIT PROCESSING FAILURES

Control: The information system:

a. Alerts designated organizational officials in the event of an audit processing failure; and
b. Takes the following additional actions: [Assignment: organization-defined actions to be taken (e.g., shut down information system, overwrite oldest audit records, stop generating audit records)].

AU-6 AUDIT REVIEW, ANALYSIS, AND REPORTING

Control: The organization:

a. Reviews and analyzes information system audit records [Assignment: organization-defined frequency] for indications of inappropriate or unusual activity, and reports findings to designated organizational officials; and
b. Adjusts the level of audit review, analysis, and reporting within the information system when there is a change in risk to organizational operations, organizational assets, individuals, other organizations, or the Nation based on law enforcement information, intelligence information, or other credible sources of information.

AU-7 AUDIT REDUCTION AND REPORT GENERATION

Control: The information system provides an audit reduction and report generation capability.

AU-8 TIME STAMPS

Control: The information system uses internal system clocks to generate time stamps for audit records.

AU-9 PROTECTION OF AUDIT INFORMATION

Control: The information system protects audit information and audit tools from unauthorized access, modification, and deletion.

AU-10 NONREPUDIATION

Control: The information system protects against an individual falsely denying having performed a particular action.

AU-11 AUDIT RECORD RETENTION

Control: The organization retains audit records for [Assignment: organization-defined time period consistent with records retention policy] to provide support for after-the-fact investigations of security incidents and to meet regulatory and organizational information retention requirements.

AU-12 AUDIT GENERATION

Control: The information system:

a. Provides audit record generation capability for the list of auditable events defined in AU-2 at [Assignment: organization-defined information system components];

b. Allows designated organizational personnel to select which auditable events are to be audited by specific components of the system; and

c. Generates audit records for the list of audited events defined in AU-2 with the content as defined in AU-3.

AU-13 MONITORING FOR INFORMATION DISCLOSURE

Control: The organization monitors open source information for evidence of unauthorized exfiltration or disclosure of organizational information [Assignment: organization-defined frequency].

AU-14 SESSION AUDIT

Control: The information system provides the capability to:

a. Capture/record and log all content related to a user session; and

b. Remotely view/hear all content related to an established user session in real time.

FAMILY: SECURITY ASSESSMENT AND AUTHORIZATION CLASS: MANAGEMENT

CA-1 SECURITY ASSESSMENT AND AUTHORIZATION POLICIES AND PROCEDURES

Control: The organization develops, disseminates, and reviews/updates [Assignment: organization-defined frequency]:

a. Formal, documented security assessment and authorization policies that address purpose, scope, roles, responsibilities, management commitment, coordination among organizational entities, and compliance; and

b. Formal, documented procedures to facilitate the implementation of the security assessment and authorization policies and associated security assessment and authorization controls.

CA-2 SECURITY ASSESSMENTS

Control: The organization:

a. Develops a security assessment plan that describes the scope of the assessment including:
- Security controls and control enhancements under assessment;
- Assessment procedures to be used to determine security control effectiveness; and
- Assessment environment, assessment team, and assessment roles and responsibilities;

b. Assesses the security controls in the information system [Assignment: organization-defined frequency] to determine the extent to which the controls are implemented correctly, operating as intended, and producing the desired outcome with respect to meeting the security requirements for the system;

c. Produces a security assessment report that documents the results of the assessment; and

d. Provides the results of the security control assessment, in writing, to the authorizing official or authorizing official's designated representative.

CA-3 INFORMATION SYSTEM CONNECTIONS

Control: The organization:

a. Authorizes connections from the information system to other information systems outside the authorization boundary through the use of interconnection security agreements;

b. Documents, for each connection, the interface characteristics, security requirements, and the nature of the information communicated; and

c. Monitors the information system connections on an ongoing basis, verifying enforcement of security requirements.

CA-4 SECURITY CERTIFICATION
[Withdrawn: Incorporated into CA-2]

CA-5 PLAN OF ACTION AND MILESTONES
Control: The organization:

a. Develops a plan of action and milestones for the information system to document the organization's planned remedial actions to correct weaknesses or deficiencies noted during the assessment of the security controls and to reduce or eliminate known vulnerabilities in the system; and

b. Updates existing plan of action and milestones [Assignment: organization-defined frequency] based on the findings from security controls' assessments, security impact analyses, and continuous monitoring activities.

CA-6 SECURITY AUTHORIZATION
Control: The organization:

a. Assigns a senior-level executive or manager to the role of authorizing official for the information system;

b. Ensures that the authorizing official authorizes the information system for processing before commencing operations; and

c. Updates the security authorization [Assignment: organization-defined frequency].

CA-7 CONTINUOUS MONITORING
Control: The organization establishes a continuous monitoring strategy and implements a continuous monitoring program that includes:

a. A configuration management process for the information system and its constituent components;

b. A determination of the security impact of changes to the information system and environment of operation;

c. Ongoing security control assessments in accordance with the organizational continuous monitoring strategy; and

d. Reporting the security state of the information system to appropriate organizational officials [Assignment: organization-defined frequency].

CA-7(1) CONTINUOUS MONITORING (Control Enhancement)

Control: The organization employs an independent assessor or assessment team to monitor the security controls in the information system on an ongoing basis.

FAMILY: CONFIGURATION MANAGEMENT
CLASS: OPERATIONAL

CM-1 CONFIGURATION MANAGEMENT POLICY AND PROCEDURES
Control: The organization develops, disseminates, and reviews/updates [Assignment: organization-defined frequency]:

  a. A formal, documented configuration management policy that addresses purpose, scope, roles, responsibilities, management commitment, coordination among organizational entities, and compliance; and
  b. Formal, documented procedures to facilitate the implementation of the configuration management policy and associated configuration management controls.

CM-2 BASELINE CONFIGURATION
Control: The organization develops, documents, and maintains under configuration control a current baseline configuration of the information system.

CM-3 CONFIGURATION CHANGE CONTROL
Control: The organization:

  a. Determines the types of changes to the information system that are configuration controlled;
  b. Approves configuration-controlled changes to the system with explicit consideration for security impact analyses;
  c. Documents approved configuration-controlled changes to the system;
  d. Retains and reviews records of configuration-controlled changes to the system;
  e. Audits activities associated with configuration-controlled changes to the system; and
  f. Coordinates and provides oversight for configuration change control activities through [Assignment: organization-defined configuration change control element (e.g., committee, board)]

that convenes [Selection: (one or more): [Assignment: organization-defined frequency]; [Assignment: organization-defined configuration change conditions]].

CM-4 SECURITY IMPACT ANALYSIS

Control: The organization analyzes changes to the information system to determine potential security impacts prior to change implementation.

CM-5 ACCESS RESTRICTIONS FOR CHANGE

Control: The organization defines, documents, approves, and enforces physical and logical access restrictions associated with changes to the information system.

CM-6 CONFIGURATION SETTINGS

Control: The organization:

a. Establishes and documents mandatory configuration settings for information technology products employed within the information system using [Assignment: organization-defined security configuration checklists] that reflect the most restrictive mode consistent with operational requirements;
b. Implements the configuration settings;
c. Identifies, documents, and approves exceptions from the mandatory configuration settings for individual components within the information system based on explicit operational requirements; and
d. Monitors and controls changes to the configuration settings in accordance with organizational policies and procedures.

CM-7 LEAST FUNCTIONALITY

Control: The organization configures the information system to provide only essential capabilities and specifically prohibits or restricts the use of the following functions, ports, protocols, and/or services: [Assignment: organization-defined list of prohibited or restricted functions, ports, protocols, and/or services].

CM-8 INFORMATION SYSTEM COMPONENT INVENTORY

Control: The organization develops, documents, and maintains an inventory of information system components that:

a. Accurately reflects the current information system;

b. Is consistent with the authorization boundary of the information system;

c. Is at the level of granularity deemed necessary for tracking and reporting;

d. Includes [Assignment: organization-defined information deemed necessary to achieve effective property accountability]; and

e. Is available for review and audit by designated organizational officials.

CM-9 CONFIGURATION MANAGEMENT PLAN

Control: The organization develops, documents, and implements a configuration management plan for the information system that:

a. Addresses roles, responsibilities, and configuration management processes and procedures;

b. Defines the configuration items for the information system and when in the system development life cycle the configuration items are placed under configuration management; and

c. Establishes the means for identifying configuration items throughout the system development life cycle and a process for managing the configuration of the configuration items.

FAMILY: CONTINGENCY PLANNING
CLASS: OPERATIONAL

CP-1 CONTINGENCY PLANNING POLICY AND PROCEDURES

Control: The organization develops, disseminates, and reviews/updates [Assignment: organization-defined frequency]:

a. A formal, documented contingency planning policy that addresses purpose, scope, roles, responsibilities, management commitment, coordination among organizational entities, and compliance; and

b. Formal, documented procedures to facilitate the implementation of the contingency planning policy and associated contingency planning controls.

CP-2 CONTINGENCY PLAN

Control: The organization:

a. Develops a contingency plan for the information system that:
   - Identifies essential missions and business functions and associated contingency requirements;
   - Provides recovery objectives, restoration priorities, and metrics;
   - Addresses contingency roles, responsibilities, and assigned individuals with contact information;
   - Addresses maintaining essential missions and business functions despite an information system disruption, compromise, or failure;
   - Addresses eventual full information system restoration without deterioration of the security measures originally planned and implemented; and
   - Is reviewed and approved by designated officials within the organization;

b. Distributes copies of the contingency plan to [Assignment: organization-defined list of key contingency personnel (identified by name and/or by role) and organizational elements];

c. Coordinates contingency planning activities with incident handling activities;

d. Reviews the contingency plan for the information system [Assignment: organization-defined frequency];

e. Revises the contingency plan to address changes to the organization, information system, or environment of operation and problems encountered during contingency plan implementation, execution, or testing; and

f. Communicates contingency plan changes to [Assignment: organization-defined list of key contingency personnel (identified by name and/or by role) and organizational elements].

CP-3 CONTINGENCY TRAINING

Control: The organization trains personnel in their contingency roles and responsibilities with respect to the information system and provides refresher training [Assignment: organization-defined frequency].

CP-4 CONTINGENCY PLAN TESTING AND EXERCISES

Control: The organization:

a. Tests and/or exercises the contingency plan for the information system [Assignment: organization-defined frequency] using [Assignment: organization-defined tests and/or exercises] to determine the plan's effectiveness and the organization's readiness to execute the plan; and

b. Reviews the contingency plan test/exercise results and initiates corrective actions.

CP-5 CONTINGENCY PLAN UPDATE
[Withdrawn Incorporated into CP-2]

CP-6 ALTERNATE STORAGE SITE
Control: The organization establishes an alternate storage site including necessary agreements to permit the storage and recovery of information system backup information.

CP-7 ALTERNATE PROCESSING SITE
Control: The organization:

a. Establishes an alternate processing site including necessary agreements to permit the resumption of information system operations for essential missions and business functions within [Assignment: organization-defined time period consistent with recovery time objectives] when the primary processing capabilities are unavailable; and

b. Ensures that equipment and supplies required to resume operations are available at the alternate site or contracts are in place to support delivery to the site in time to support the organization-defined time period for resumption.

CP-8 TELECOMMUNICATIONS SERVICES
Control: The organization establishes alternate telecommunications services including necessary agreements to permit the resumption of information system operations for essential missions and business functions within [Assignment: organization-defined time period] when the primary telecommunications capabilities are unavailable.

CP-9 INFORMATION SYSTEM BACKUP
Control: The organization:

a. Conducts backups of user-level information contained in the information system [Assignment: organization-defined frequency consistent with recovery time and recovery point objectives];

b. Conducts backups of system-level information contained in the information system [Assignment: organization-defined frequency consistent with recovery time and recovery point objectives];

c. Conducts backups of information system documentation including security-related documentation [Assignment: organization-defined frequency consistent with recovery time and recovery point objectives]; and

d. Protects the confidentiality and integrity of backup information at the storage location.

CP-10 INFORMATION SYSTEM RECOVERY AND RECONSTITUTION

Control: The organization provides for the recovery and reconstitution of the information system to a known state after a disruption, compromise, or failure.

FAMILY: IDENTIFICATION AND AUTHENTICATION CLASS: TECHNICAL

IA-1 IDENTIFICATION AND AUTHENTICATION POLICY AND PROCEDURES

Control: The organization develops, disseminates, and reviews/updates [Assignment: organization-defined frequency]:

a. A formal, documented identification and authentication policy that addresses purpose, scope, roles, responsibilities, management commitment, coordination among organizational entities, and compliance; and

b. Formal, documented procedures to facilitate the implementation of the identification and authentication policy and associated identification and authentication controls.

IA-2 IDENTIFICATION AND AUTHENTICATION (ORGANIZATIONAL USERS)

Control: The information system uniquely identifies and authenticates organizational users (or processes acting on behalf of organizational users).

IA-3 DEVICE IDENTIFICATION AND AUTHENTICATION

Control: The information system uniquely identifies and authenticates [Assignment: organization-defined list of specific and/or types of devices] before establishing a connection.

IA-4 IDENTIFIER MANAGEMENT

Control: The organization manages information system identifiers for users and devices by:

a. Receiving authorization from a designated organizational official to assign a user or device identifier;
b. Selecting an identifier that uniquely identifies an individual or device;
c. Assigning the user identifier to the intended party or the device identifier to the intended device;
d. Preventing reuse of user or device identifiers for [Assignment: organization-defined time period]; and
e. Disabling the user identifier after [Assignment: organization-defined time period of inactivity].

IA-5 AUTHENTICATOR MANAGEMENT

Control: The organization manages information system authenticators for users and devices by:

a. Verifying, as part of the initial authenticator distribution, the identity of the individual and/or device receiving the authenticator;
b. Establishing initial authenticator content for authenticators defined by the organization;
c. Ensuring that authenticators have sufficient strength of mechanism for their intended use;
d. Establishing and implementing administrative procedures for initial authenticator distribution, for lost/compromised or damaged authenticators, and for revoking authenticators;
e. Changing default content of authenticators upon information system installation;
f. Establishing minimum and maximum lifetime restrictions and reuse conditions for authenticators (if appropriate);
g. Changing/refreshing authenticators [Assignment: organization-defined time period by authenticator type];

h. Protecting authenticator content from unauthorized disclosure and modification; and

i. Requiring users to take, and having devices implement, specific measures to safeguard authenticators.

IA-6 AUTHENTICATOR FEEDBACK

Control: The information system obscures feedback of authentication information during the authentication process to protect the information from possible exploitation/use by unauthorized individuals.

IA-7 CRYPTOGRAPHIC MODULE AUTHENTICATION

Control: The information system uses mechanisms for authentication to a cryptographic module that meet the requirements of applicable federal laws, Executive Orders, directives, policies, regulations, standards, and guidance for such authentication.

IA-8 IDENTIFICATION AND AUTHENTICATION (NONORGANIZATIONAL USERS)

Control: The information system uniquely identifies and authenticates nonorganizational users (or processes acting on behalf of nonorganizational users).

FAMILY: INCIDENT RESPONSE
CLASS: OPERATIONAL

IR-1 INCIDENT RESPONSE POLICY AND PROCEDURES

Control: The organization develops, disseminates, and reviews/updates [Assignment: organization-defined frequency]:

a. A formal, documented incident response policy that addresses purpose, scope, roles, responsibilities, management commitment, coordination among organizational entities, and compliance; and

b. Formal, documented procedures to facilitate the implementation of the incident response policy and associated incident response controls.

IR-2 INCIDENT RESPONSE TRAINING

Control: The organization:

a. Trains personnel in their incident response roles and responsibilities with respect to the information system; and

b. Provides refresher training [Assignment: organization-defined frequency].

IR-3 INCIDENT RESPONSE TESTING AND EXERCISES

Control: The organization tests and/or exercises the incident response capability for the information system [Assignment: organization-defined frequency] using [Assignment: organization-defined tests and/or exercises] to determine the incident response effectiveness and documents the results.

IR-4 INCIDENT HANDLING

Control: The organization:

a. Implements an incident handling capability for security incidents that includes preparation, detection and analysis, containment, eradication, and recovery;

b. Coordinates incident handling activities with contingency planning activities; and

c. Incorporates lessons learned from ongoing incident handling activities into incident response procedures, training, and testing/exercises, and implements the resulting changes accordingly.

IR-5 INCIDENT MONITORING

Control: The organization tracks and documents information system security incidents.

IR-6 INCIDENT REPORTING

Control: The organization:

a. Requires personnel to report suspected security incidents to the organizational incident response capability within [Assignment: organization-defined time-period]; and

b. Reports security incident information to designated authorities.

IR-7 INCIDENT RESPONSE ASSISTANCE

Control: The organization provides an incident response support resource, integral to the organizational incident response capability, that offers advice and assistance to users of the information system for the handling and reporting of security incidents.

IR-8 INCIDENT RESPONSE PLAN

Control: The organization:

a. Develops an incident response plan that:
- Provides the organization with a roadmap for implementing its incident response capability;
- Describes the structure and organization of the incident response capability and Special Publication 800-53 Recommended Security Controls for Federal Information Systems and Organizations
- Provides a high-level approach for how the incident response capability fits into the overall organization;
- Meets the unique requirements of the organization, which relate to mission, size, structure, and functions;
- Defines reportable incidents;
- Provides metrics for measuring the incident response capability within the organization; and
- Defines the resources and management support needed to effectively maintain and mature an incident response capability;

b. Is reviewed and approved by designated officials within the organization;

c. Distributes copies of the incident response plan to [Assignment: organization-defined list of incident response personnel (identified by name and/or by role) and organizational elements];

c. Reviews the incident response plan [Assignment: organization-defined frequency];

d. Revises the incident response plan to address system/organizational changes or problems encountered during plan implementation, execution, or testing; and

e. Communicates incident response plan changes to [Assignment: organization-defined list of incident response personnel (identified by name and/or by role) and organizational elements].

FAMILY: MAINTENANCE
CLASS: OPERATIONAL

MA-1 SYSTEM MAINTENANCE POLICY AND PROCEDURES

Control: The organization develops, disseminates, and reviews/updates [Assignment: organization-defined frequency]:

a. A formal, documented information system maintenance policy that addresses purpose, scope, roles, responsibilities, management commitment, coordination among organizational entities, and compliance; and

b. Formal, documented procedures to facilitate the implementation of the information system maintenance policy and associated system maintenance controls.

MA-2 CONTROLLED MAINTENANCE

Control: The organization:

a. Schedules, performs, documents, and reviews records of maintenance and repairs on information system components in accordance with manufacturer or vendor specifications and/or organizational requirements;

b. Controls all maintenance activities, whether performed on site or remotely and whether the equipment is serviced on site or removed to another location;

c. Requires that a designated official explicitly approve the removal of the information system or system components from organizational facilities for off-site maintenance or repairs;

d. Sanitizes equipment to remove all information from associated media prior to removal from organizational facilities for off-site maintenance or repairs; and

e. Checks all potentially impacted security controls to verify that the controls are still functioning properly following maintenance or repair actions.

MA-3 MAINTENANCE TOOLS

Control: The organization approves, controls, monitors the use of, and maintains on an ongoing basis information system maintenance tools.

MA-4 NONLOCAL MAINTENANCE

Control: The organization:

a. Authorizes, monitors, and controls nonlocal maintenance and diagnostic activities;

b. Allows the use of nonlocal maintenance and diagnostic tools only as consistent with organizational policy and documented in the security plan for the information system;

    c. Employs strong identification and authentication techniques in the establishment of nonlocal maintenance and diagnostic sessions;

    d. Maintains records for nonlocal maintenance and diagnostic activities; and

    e. Terminates all sessions and network connections when nonlocal maintenance is completed.

MA-5 MAINTENANCE PERSONNEL

Control: The organization:

    a. Establishes a process for maintenance personnel authorization and maintains a current list of authorized maintenance organizations or personnel; and

    b. Ensures that personnel performing maintenance on the information system have required access authorizations or designates organizational personnel with required access authorizations and technical competence deemed necessary to supervise information system maintenance when maintenance personnel do not possess the required access authorizations.

MA-6 TIMELY MAINTENANCE

Control: The organization obtains maintenance support and/or spare parts for [Assignment: organization-defined list of security-critical information system components and/or key information technology components] within [Assignment: organization-defined time period] of failure.

FAMILY: MEDIA PROTECTION
CLASS: OPERATIONAL

MP-1 MEDIA PROTECTION POLICY AND PROCEDURES

Control: The organization develops, disseminates, and reviews/updates [Assignment: organization-defined frequency]:

    a. A formal, documented media protection policy that addresses purpose, scope, roles, responsibilities, management commitment, coordination among organizational entities, and compliance; and

b. Formal, documented procedures to facilitate the implementation of the media protection policy and associated media protection controls.

MP-2 MEDIA ACCESS

Control: The organization restricts access to [Assignment: organization-defined types of digital and nondigital media] to [Assignment: organization-defined list of authorized individuals] using [Assignment: organization-defined security measures].

MP-3 MEDIA MARKING

Control: The organization:

a. Marks, in accordance with organizational policies and procedures, removable information system media and information system output indicating the distribution limitations, handling caveats, and applicable security markings (if any) of the information; and

b. Exempts [Assignment: organization-defined list of removable media types] from marking as long as the exempted items remain within [Assignment: organization-defined controlled areas].

MP-4 MEDIA STORAGE

Control: The organization:

a. Physically controls and securely stores [Assignment: organization-defined types of digital and nondigital media] within [Assignment: organization-defined controlled areas] using [Assignment: organization-defined security measures];

b. Protects information system media until the media are destroyed or sanitized using approved equipment, techniques, and procedures.

MP-5 MEDIA TRANSPORT

Control: The organization:

a. Protects and controls [Assignment: organization-defined types of digital and nondigital media] during transport outside controlled areas using [Assignment: organization-defined security measures];

b. Maintains accountability for information system media during transport outside controlled areas; and

c. Restricts the activities associated with transport of such media to authorized personnel.

MP-6 MEDIA SANITIZATION

Control: The organization:

a. Sanitizes information system media, both digital and non-digital, prior to disposal, release out of organizational control, or release for reuse; and

b. Employs sanitization mechanisms with strength and integrity commensurate with the classification or sensitivity of the information.

FAMILY: PHYSICAL AND ENVIRONMENTAL PROTECTION
CLASS: OPERATIONAL

PE-1 PHYSICAL AND ENVIRONMENTAL PROTECTION POLICY AND PROCEDURES

Control: The organization develops, disseminates, and reviews/updates [Assignment: organization-defined frequency]:

a. A formal, documented physical and environmental protection policy that addresses purpose, scope, roles, responsibilities, management commitment, coordination among organizational entities, and compliance; and

b. Formal, documented procedures to facilitate the implementation of the physical and environmental protection policy and associated physical and environmental protection controls.

PE-2 PHYSICAL ACCESS AUTHORIZATIONS

Control: The organization:

a. Develops and keeps current a list of personnel with authorized access to the facility where the information system resides (except for those areas within the facility officially designated as publicly accessible);

b. Issues authorization credentials; and

c. Reviews and approves the access list and authorization credentials [Assignment: organization-defined frequency], removing from the access list personnel no longer requiring access.

PE-3 PHYSICAL ACCESS CONTROL

Control: The organization:

a. Enforces physical access authorizations for all physical access points (including designated entry/exit points) to the facility where the information system resides (excluding those areas within the facility officially designated as publicly accessible);
b. Verifies individual access authorizations before granting access to the facility;
c. Controls entry to the facility containing the information system using physical access devices and/or guards;
d. Controls access to areas officially designated as publicly accessible in accordance with the organization's assessment of risk;
e. Secures keys, combinations, and other physical access devices;
f. Inventories physical access devices [Assignment: organization-defined frequency]; and
g. Changes combinations and keys [Assignment: organization-defined frequency] and when keys are lost, combinations are compromised, or individuals are transferred or terminated.

PE-4 ACCESS CONTROL FOR TRANSMISSION MEDIUM

Control: The organization controls physical access to information system distribution and transmission lines within organizational facilities.

PE-5 ACCESS CONTROL FOR OUTPUT DEVICES

Control: The organization controls physical access to information system output devices to prevent unauthorized individuals from obtaining the output.

PE-6 MONITORING PHYSICAL ACCESS

Control: The organization:

a. Monitors physical access to the information system to detect and respond to physical security incidents;
b. Reviews physical access logs [Assignment: organization-defined frequency]; and

c. Coordinates results of reviews and investigations with the organization's incident response capability.

PE-7 VISITOR CONTROL

Control: The organization controls physical access to the information system by authenticating visitors before authorizing access to the facility where the information system resides other than areas designated as publicly accessible.

PE-8 ACCESS RECORDS

Control: The organization:

a. Maintains visitor access records to the facility where the information system resides (except for those areas within the facility officially designated as publicly accessible); and

b. Reviews visitor access records [Assignment: organization-defined frequency].

PE-9 POWER EQUIPMENT AND POWER CABLING

Control: The organization protects power equipment and power cabling for the information system from damage and destruction.

PE-10 EMERGENCY SHUTOFF

Control: The organization:

a. Provides the capability of shutting off power to the information system or individual system components in emergency situations;

b. Places emergency shutoff switches or devices in [Assignment: organization-defined location by information system or system component] to facilitate safe and easy access for personnel; and

c. Protects emergency power shutoff capability from unauthorized activation.

PE-11 EMERGENCY POWER

Control: The organization provides a short-term uninterruptible power supply to facilitate an orderly shutdown of the information system in the event of a primary power source loss.

PE-12 EMERGENCY LIGHTING

Control: The organization employs and maintains automatic emergency lighting for the information system that activates in the event of a power outage or disruption and that covers emergency exits and evacuation routes within the facility.

PE-13 FIRE PROTECTION

Control: The organization employs and maintains fire suppression and detection devices/systems for the information system that are supported by an independent energy source.

PE-14 TEMPERATURE AND HUMIDITY CONTROLS

Control: The organization:

a. Maintains temperature and humidity levels within the facility where the information system resides at [Assignment: organization-defined acceptable levels]; and
b. Monitors temperature and humidity levels [Assignment: organization-defined frequency].

PE-15 WATER DAMAGE PROTECTION

Control: The organization protects the information system from damage resulting from water leakage by providing master shutoff valves that are accessible, working properly, and known to key personnel.

PE-16 DELIVERY AND REMOVAL

Control: The organization authorizes, monitors, and controls [Assignment: organization-defined types of information system components] entering and exiting the facility and maintains records of those items.

PE-17 ALTERNATE WORK SITE

Control: The organization:

a. Employs [Assignment: organization-defined management, operational, and technical information system security controls] at alternate work sites;
b. Assesses, as feasible, the effectiveness of security controls at alternate work sites; and
c. Provides a means for employees to communicate with information security personnel in case of security incidents or problems.

PE-18 LOCATION OF INFORMATION SYSTEM COMPONENTS

Control: The organization positions information system components within the facility to minimize potential damage from physical and environmental hazards and to minimize the opportunity for unauthorized access.

PE-19 INFORMATION LEAKAGE
Control: The organization protects the information system from information leakage due to electromagnetic signals' emanations.

FAMILY: PLANNING
CLASS: MANAGEMENT

PL-1 SECURITY PLANNING POLICY AND PROCEDURES
Control: The organization develops, disseminates, and reviews/updates [Assignment: organization-defined frequency]:

    a. A formal, documented security planning policy that addresses purpose, scope, roles, responsibilities, management commitment, coordination among organizational entities, and compliance; and

    b. Formal, documented procedures to facilitate the implementation of the security planning policy and associated security planning controls.

PL-2 SYSTEM SECURITY PLAN
Control: The organization:

    a. Develops a security plan for the information system that:
- Is consistent with the organization's enterprise architecture;
- Explicitly defines the authorization boundary for the system;
- Describes the operational context of the information system in terms of missions and business processes;
- Provides the security categorization of the information system including supporting rationale;
- Describes the operational environment for the information system;
- Describes relationships with or connections to other information systems;
- Provides an overview of the security requirements for the system;
- Describes the security controls in place or planned for meeting those requirements, including a rationale for the tailoring and supplementation decisions; and

- Is reviewed and approved by the authorizing official or designated representative prior to plan implementation;
  b. Reviews the security plan for the information system [Assignment: organization-defined frequency]; and
  c. Updates the plan to address changes to the information system/environment of operation or problems identified during plan implementation or security control assessments.

PL-3 SYSTEM SECURITY PLAN UPDATE
[Withdrawn: Incorporated into PL-2]

PL-4 RULES OF BEHAVIOR
Control: The organization:

a. Establishes and makes readily available to all information system users the rules that describe their responsibilities and expected behavior with regard to information and information system usage and Special Publication 800-53 Recommended Security Controls for Federal Information Systems and Organizations; and
b. Receives signed acknowledgment from users indicating that they have read, understand, and agree to abide by the rules of behavior, before authorizing access to information and the information system.

PL-5 PRIVACY IMPACT ASSESSMENT
Control: The organization conducts a privacy impact assessment on the information system in accordance with OMB policy.

PL-6 SECURITY-RELATED ACTIVITY PLANNING
Control: The organization plans and coordinates security-related activities affecting the information system before conducting such activities in order to reduce the impact on organizational operations (i.e., mission, functions, image, and reputation), organizational assets, and individuals.

FAMILY: PERSONNEL SECURITY
CLASS: OPERATIONAL

PS-1 PERSONNEL SECURITY POLICY AND PROCEDURES
Control: The organization develops, disseminates, and reviews/updates [Assignment: organization-defined frequency]:

a. A formal, documented personnel security policy that addresses purpose, scope, roles, responsibilities, management commitment, coordination among organizational entities, and compliance; and

b. Formal, documented procedures to facilitate the implementation of the personnel security policy and associated personnel security controls.

PS-2 POSITION CATEGORIZATION

Control: The organization:

a. Assigns a risk designation to all positions;

b. Establishes screening criteria for individuals filling those positions; and

c. Reviews and revises position risk designations [Assignment: organization-defined frequency].

PS-3 PERSONNEL SCREENING

Control: The organization:

a. Screens individuals prior to authorizing access to the information system and Special Publication 800-53 Recommended Security Controls for Federal Information Systems and Organizations; and

b. Rescreens individuals according to [Assignment: organization-defined list of conditions requiring rescreening and, where rescreening is so indicated, the frequency of such rescreening].

PS-4 PERSONNEL TERMINATION

Control: The organization, upon termination of individual employment:

a. Terminates information system access;

b. Conducts exit interviews;

c. Retrieves all security-related organizational information system-related property; and

d. Retains access to organizational information and information systems formerly controlled by terminated individual.

PS-5 PERSONNEL TRANSFER

Control: The organization reviews logical and physical access authorizations to information systems/facilities when personnel are reassigned or transferred to other positions within the organization and initiates [Assignment: organization-defined transfer or reassignment actions] within [Assignment: organization-defined time period following the formal transfer action].

PS-6 ACCESS AGREEMENTS

Control: The organization:

a. Ensures that individuals requiring access to organizational information and information systems sign appropriate access agreements prior to being granted access; and
b. Reviews/updates the access agreements [Assignment: organization-defined frequency].

PS-7 THIRD-PARTY PERSONNEL SECURITY

Control: The organization:

a. Establishes personnel security requirements including security roles and responsibilities for third-party providers;
b. Documents personnel security requirements; and
c. Monitors provider compliance.

PS-8 PERSONNEL SANCTIONS

Control: The organization employs a formal sanctions process for personnel failing to comply with established information security policies and procedures.

FAMILY: RISK ASSESSMENT
CLASS: MANAGEMENT

RA-1 RISK ASSESSMENT POLICY AND PROCEDURES

Control: The organization develops, disseminates, and reviews/updates [Assignment: organization-defined frequency]:

a. A formal, documented risk assessment policy that addresses purpose, scope, roles, responsibilities, management commitment, coordination among organizational entities, and compliance; and
b. Formal, documented procedures to facilitate the implementation of the risk assessment policy and associated risk assessment controls.

RA-2 SECURITY CATEGORIZATION

Control: The organization:

a. Categorizes information and the information system in accordance with applicable federal laws, Executive Orders, directives, policies, regulations, standards, and guidance;

b. Documents the security categorization results (including supporting rationale) in the security plan for the information system; and

c. Ensures the security categorization decision is reviewed and approved by the authorizing official or authorizing official-designated representative.

RA-3 RISK ASSESSMENT

Control: The organization:

a. Conducts an assessment of risk, including the likelihood and magnitude of harm, from the unauthorized access, use, disclosure, disruption, modification, or destruction of the information system and the information it processes, stores, or transmits;

b. Documents risk assessment results in [Selection: security plan; risk assessment report; [Assignment: organization-defined document]];

c. Reviews risk assessment results [Assignment: organization-defined frequency]; and

d. Updates the risk assessment [Assignment: organization-defined frequency] or whenever there are significant changes to the information system or environment of operation (including the identification of new threats and vulnerabilities), or other conditions that may impact the security state of the system.

RA-4 RISK ASSESSMENT UPDATE

[Withdrawn: Incorporated into RA-3]

RA-5 VULNERABILITY SCANNING

Control: The organization:

a. Scans for vulnerabilities in the information system and hosted applications [Assignment: organization-defined frequency and/or randomly in accordance with organization-defined process] and when new vulnerabilities potentially affecting the system/applications are identified and reported;

b. Employs vulnerability scanning tools and techniques that promote interoperability among tools and automate parts of the vulnerability management process by using standards for:
- Enumerating platforms, software flaws, and improper configurations;
- Formatting and making transparent, checklists and test procedures; and
- Measuring vulnerability impact;

c. Analyzes vulnerability scan reports and results from security control assessments;

d. Remediates legitimate vulnerabilities [Assignment: organization-defined response times] in accordance with an organizational assessment of risk; and

e. Shares information obtained from the vulnerability scanning process and security control assessments with designated personnel throughout the organization to help eliminate similar vulnerabilities in other information systems (i.e., systemic weaknesses or deficiencies).

FAMILY: SYSTEM AND SERVICES ACQUISITION
CLASS: MANAGEMENT

SA-1 SYSTEM AND SERVICES ACQUISITION POLICY AND PROCEDURES

Control: The organization develops, disseminates, and reviews/updates [Assignment: organization-defined frequency]:

a. A formal, documented system and services acquisition policy that includes information on security considerations and that addresses purpose, scope, roles, responsibilities, management commitment, coordination among organizational entities, and compliance; and

b. Formal, documented procedures to facilitate the implementation of the system and services acquisition policy and associated system and services acquisition controls.

SA-2 ALLOCATION OF RESOURCES

Control: The organization:

a. Includes a determination of information security requirements for the information system in mission/business process planning;

b. Determines, documents, and allocates the resources required to protect the information system as part of its capital planning and investment control process; and

c. Establishes a discrete line item for information security in organizational programming and budgeting documentation.

SA-3 LIFE CYCLE SUPPORT
Control: The organization:

a. Manages the information system using a system development life cycle methodology that includes information security considerations;

b. Defines and documents information system security roles and responsibilities throughout the system development life cycle; and

c. Identifies individuals having information system security roles and responsibilities.

SA-4 ACQUISITIONS
Control: The organization includes the following requirements and/or specifications, explicitly or by reference, in information system acquisition contracts based on an assessment of risk and in accordance with applicable federal laws, Executive Orders, directives, policies, regulations, and standards:

a. Security functional requirements/specifications;

b. Security-related documentation requirements; and

c. Developmental and evaluation-related assurance requirements.

SA-5 INFORMATION SYSTEM DOCUMENTATION
Control: The organization:

a. Obtains, protects as required, and makes available to authorized personnel, administrator documentation for the information system that describes:
  - Secure configuration, installation, and operation of the information system;
  - Effective use and maintenance of security features/functions; and
  - Known vulnerabilities regarding configuration and use of administrative (i.e., privileged) functions;

b. Obtains, protects as required, and makes available to authorized personnel user documentation for the information system that describes:
- User-accessible security features/functions and how to effectively use those security features/functions;
- Methods for user interaction with the information system, which enable individuals to use the system in a more secure manner; and
- User responsibilities in maintaining the security of the information and information system;

c. Documents attempts to obtain information system documentation when such documentation is either unavailable or nonexistent.

SA-6 SOFTWARE USAGE RESTRICTIONS
Control: The organization:

a. Uses software and associated documentation in accordance with contract agreements and copyright laws;
b. Employs tracking systems for software and associated documentation protected by quantity licenses to control copying and distribution; and
c. Controls and documents the use of peer-to-peer file sharing technology to ensure that this capability is not used for the unauthorized distribution, display, performance, or reproduction of copyrighted work.

SA-7 USER-INSTALLED SOFTWARE
Control: The organization enforces explicit rules governing the installation of software by users.

SA-8 SECURITY ENGINEERING PRINCIPLES
Control: The organization applies information system security engineering principles in the specification, design, development, implementation, and modification of the information system.

SA-9 EXTERNAL INFORMATION SYSTEM SERVICES
Control: The organization:

a. Requires that providers of external information system services comply with organizational information security requirements and employ appropriate security controls in accordance with applicable federal laws, Executive Orders, directives, policies, regulations, standards, and guidance;

b. Defines and documents government oversight and user roles and responsibilities with regard to external information system services; and

c. Monitors security control compliance by external service providers.

SA-10 DEVELOPER CONFIGURATION MANAGEMENT

Control: The organization requires that information system developers/integrators:

a. Perform configuration management during information system design, development, implementation, and operation;

b. Manage and control changes to the information system;

c. Implement only organization-approved changes;

d. Document approved changes to the information system; and

e. Track security flaws and flaw resolution.

SA-11 DEVELOPER SECURITY TESTING

Control: The organization requires that information system developers/integrators, in consultation with associated security personnel (including security engineers):

a. Create and implement a security test and evaluation plan;

b. Implement a verifiable flaw remediation process to correct weaknesses and deficiencies identified during the security testing and evaluation process; and

c. Document the results of the security testing/evaluation and flaw remediation processes.

SA-12 SUPPLY CHAIN PROTECTION

Control: The organization protects against supply chain threats by employing: [Assignment: organization-defined list of measures to protect against supply chain threats] as part of a comprehensive, defense-in-breadth information security strategy.

SA-13 TRUSTWORTHINESS

Control: The organization requires that the information system meets [Assignment: organization-defined level of trustworthiness].

SA-14 CRITICAL INFORMATION SYSTEM COMPONENTS

Control: The organization:

a. Determines [Assignment: organization-defined list of critical information system components that require reimplementation]; and

b. Reimplements or custom develops such information system components.

FAMILY: SYSTEM AND COMMUNICATIONS PROTECTION
CLASS: TECHNICAL

SC-1 SYSTEM AND COMMUNICATIONS PROTECTION POLICY AND PROCEDURES

Control: The organization develops, disseminates, and reviews/updates [Assignment: organization-defined frequency]:

a. A formal, documented system and communications protection policy that addresses purpose, scope, roles, responsibilities, management commitment, coordination among organizational entities, and compliance; and

b. Formal, documented procedures to facilitate the implementation of the system and communications protection policy and associated system and communications protection controls.

SC-2 APPLICATION PARTITIONING

Control: The information system separates user functionality (including user interface services) from information system management functionality.

SC-3 SECURITY FUNCTION ISOLATION

Control: The information system isolates security functions from nonsecurity functions.

SC-4 INFORMATION IN SHARED RESOURCES

Control: The information system prevents unauthorized and unintended information transfer via shared system resources.

SC-5 DENIAL OF SERVICE PROTECTION

Control: The information system protects against or limits the effects of the following types of denial of service attacks: [Assignment: organization-defined list of types of denial of service attacks or reference to source for current list].

SC-6 RESOURCE PRIORITY

Control: The information system limits the use of resources by priority.

SC-7 BOUNDARY PROTECTION

Control: The information system:

a. Monitors and controls communications at the external boundary of the system and at key internal boundaries within the system; and

b. Connects to external networks or information systems only through managed interfaces consisting of boundary protection devices arranged in accordance with an organizational security architecture.

SC-8 TRANSMISSION INTEGRITY

Control: The information system protects the integrity of transmitted information.

SC-9 TRANSMISSION CONFIDENTIALITY

Control: The information system protects the confidentiality of transmitted information.

SC-10 NETWORK DISCONNECT

Control: The information system terminates the network connection associated with a communications session at the end of the session or after [Assignment: organization-defined time period] of inactivity.

SC-11 TRUSTED PATH

Control: The information system establishes a trusted communications path between the user and the following security functions of the system: [Assignment: organization-defined security functions to include, at a minimum, information system authentication and reauthentication].

SC-12 CRYPTOGRAPHIC KEY ESTABLISHMENT AND MANAGEMENT

Control: The organization establishes and manages cryptographic keys for required cryptography employed within the information system.

SC-13 USE OF CRYPTOGRAPHY

Control: The information system implements required cryptographic protections using cryptographic modules that comply with applicable federal laws, Executive Orders, directives, policies, regulations, standards, and guidance.

SC-14 PUBLIC ACCESS PROTECTIONS

Control: The information system protects the integrity and availability of publicly available information and applications.

SC-15 COLLABORATIVE COMPUTING DEVICES

Control: The information system:

a. Prohibits remote activation of collaborative computing devices with the following exceptions: [Assignment: organization-defined exceptions where remote activation is to be allowed]; and
b. Provides an explicit indication of use to users physically present at the devices.

SC-16 TRANSMISSION OF SECURITY ATTRIBUTES

Control: The information system associates security attributes with information exchanged between information systems.

SC-17 PUBLIC KEY INFRASTRUCTURE CERTIFICATES

Control: The organization issues public key certificates under an [Assignment: organization-defined certificate policy] or obtains public key certificates under an appropriate certificate policy from an approved service provider.

SC-18 MOBILE CODE

Control: The organization:

a. Defines acceptable and unacceptable mobile code and mobile code technologies;

b. Establishes usage restrictions and implementation guidance for acceptable mobile code and mobile code technologies; and

c. Authorizes, monitors, and controls the use of mobile code within the information system.

SC-19 VOICE OVER INTERNET PROTOCOL

Control: The organization:

a. Establishes usage restrictions and implementation guidance for Voice over Internet Protocol (VoIP) technologies based on the potential to cause damage to the information system if used maliciously; and

b. Authorizes, monitors, and controls the use of VoIP within the information system.

SC-20 SECURE NAME/ADDRESS RESOLUTION SERVICE (AUTHORITATIVE SOURCE)

Control: The information system provides additional data origin and integrity artifacts along with the authoritative data the system returns in response to name/address resolution queries.

SC-21 SECURE NAME/ADDRESS RESOLUTION SERVICE (RECURSIVE OR CACHING RESOLVER)

Control: The information system performs data origin authentication and data integrity verification on the name/address resolution responses the system receives from authoritative sources when requested by client systems.

SC-22 ARCHITECTURE AND PROVISIONING FOR NAME/ADDRESS RESOLUTION SERVICE

Control: The information systems that collectively provide name/address resolution service for an organization are fault tolerant and implement internal/external role separation.

SC-23 SESSION AUTHENTICITY

Control: The information system provides mechanisms to protect the authenticity of communications sessions.

SC-24 FAIL IN KNOWN STATE

Control: The information system fails to a [Assignment: organization-defined known state] for [Assignment: organization-defined types of failures] preserving [Assignment: organization-defined system state information] in failure.

SC-25 THIN NODES

Control: The information system employs processing components that have minimal functionality and information storage.

SC-26 HONEYPOTS

Control: The information system includes components specifically designed to be the target of malicious attacks for the purpose of detecting, deflecting, and analyzing such attacks.

SC-27 OPERATING SYSTEM-INDEPENDENT APPLICATIONS

Control: The information system includes: [Assignment: organization-defined operating system independent applications].

SC-28 PROTECTION OF INFORMATION AT REST

Control: The information system protects the confidentiality and integrity of information at rest.

SC-29 HETEROGENEITY

Control: The organization employs diverse information technologies in the implementation of the information system.

SC-30 VIRTUALIZATION TECHNIQUES

Control: The organization employs virtualization techniques to present information system components as other types of components, or components with differing configurations.

SC-31 COVERT CHANNEL ANALYSIS

Control: The organization requires that information system developers/integrators perform a covert channel analysis to identify those aspects of system communication that are potential avenues for covert storage and timing channels.

SC-32 INFORMATION SYSTEM PARTITIONING

Control: The organization partitions the information system into components residing in separate physical domains (or environments) as deemed necessary.

SC-33 TRANSMISSION PREPARATION INTEGRITY

Control: The information system protects the integrity of information during the processes of data aggregation, packaging, and transformation in preparation for transmission.

SC-34 NONMODIFIABLE EXECUTABLE PROGRAMS

Control: The information system at [Assignment: organization-defined information system components]:

a. Loads and executes the operating environment from hardware-enforced, read-only media; and
b. Loads and executes [Assignment: organization-defined applications] from hardware-enforced, read-only media.

FAMILY: SYSTEM AND INFORMATION INTEGRITY CLASS: OPERATIONAL

SI-1 SYSTEM AND INFORMATION INTEGRITY POLICY AND PROCEDURES

Control: The organization develops, disseminates, and reviews/updates [Assignment: organization defined frequency]:

a. A formal, documented system and information integrity policy that addresses purpose, scope, roles, responsibilities, management commitment, coordination among organizational entities, and compliance; and
b. Formal, documented procedures to facilitate the implementation of the system and information integrity policy and associated system and information integrity controls.

SI-2 FLAW REMEDIATION

Control: The organization:

a. Identifies, reports, and corrects information system flaws;
b. Tests software updates related to flaw remediation for effectiveness and potential side effects on organizational information systems before installation; and
c. Incorporates flaw remediation into the organizational configuration management process.

SI-3 MALICIOUS CODE PROTECTION
Control: The organization:

a. Employs malicious code protection mechanisms at information system entry and exit points and at workstations, servers, or mobile computing devices on the network to detect and eradicate malicious code:
- Transported by electronic mail, electronic mail attachments, web accesses, removable media, or other common means; or
- Inserted through the exploitation of information system vulnerabilities;

b. Updates malicious code protection mechanisms (including signature definitions) whenever new releases are available in accordance with organizational configuration management policy and procedures;

c. Configures malicious code protection mechanisms to:
- Perform periodic scans of the information system [Assignment: organization-defined frequency] and real-time scans of files from external sources as the files are downloaded, opened, or executed in accordance with organizational security policy; and
- [Selection (one or more): block malicious code; quarantine malicious code; send alert to administrator; [Assignment: organization-defined action]] in response to malicious code detection; and

d. Addresses the receipt of false positives during malicious code detection and eradication and the resulting potential impact on the availability of the information system.

SI-4 INFORMATION SYSTEM MONITORING
Control: The organization:

a. Monitors events on the information system in accordance with [Assignment: organization-defined monitoring objectives] and detects information system attacks;

b. Identifies unauthorized use of the information system;

c. Deploys monitoring devices: (i) strategically within the information system to collect organization-determined essential information; and (ii) at ad hoc locations within the system to track specific types of transactions of interest to the organization;

d. Heightens the level of information system monitoring activity whenever there is an indication of increased risk to organizational operations and assets, individuals, other organizations, or the Nation based on law enforcement information, intelligence information, or other credible sources of information; and

e. Obtains legal opinion with regard to information system monitoring activities in accordance with applicable federal laws, Executive Orders, directives, policies, or regulations.

SI-5 SECURITY ALERTS, ADVISORIES, AND DIRECTIVES
Control: The organization:

a. Receives information system security alerts, advisories, and directives from designated external organizations on an ongoing basis;

b. Generates internal security alerts, advisories, and directives as deemed necessary;

c. Disseminates security alerts, advisories, and directives to [Assignment: organization-defined list of personnel (identified by name and/or by role)]; and

d. Implements security directives in accordance with established time frames, or notifies the issuing organization of the degree of noncompliance.

SI-6 SECURITY FUNCTIONALITY VERIFICATION
Control: The information system verifies the correct operation of security functions [Selection (one or more): [Assignment: organization-defined system transitional states]; upon command by user with appropriate privilege; periodically every [Assignment: organization-defined time period]] and [Selection (one or more): notifies system administrator; shuts the system down; restarts the system; [Assignment: organization-defined alternative action(s)]] when anomalies are discovered.

SI-7 SOFTWARE AND INFORMATION INTEGRITY
Control: The information system detects unauthorized changes to software and information.

SI-8 SPAM PROTECTION
Control: The organization:

a. Employs spam protection mechanisms at information system entry and exit points at workstations, servers, or mobile computing devices on the network to detect and take action on unsolicited messages transported by electronic mail, electronic mail attachments, web accesses, or other common means; and

b. Updates spam protection mechanisms (including signature definitions) when new releases are available in accordance with organizational configuration management policy and procedures.

SI-9 INFORMATION INPUT RESTRICTIONS
Control: The organization restricts the capability to input information to the information system to authorized personnel.

SI-10 INFORMATION INPUT VALIDATION
Control: The information system checks the validity of information inputs.

SI-11 ERROR HANDLING
Control: The information system:

a. Identifies potentially security-relevant error conditions;

b. Generates error messages that provide information necessary for corrective actions without revealing [Assignment: organization-defined sensitive or potentially harmful information] in error logs and administrative messages that could be exploited by adversaries; and

c. Reveals error messages only to authorized personnel.

SI-12 INFORMATION OUTPUT HANDLING AND RETENTION
Control: The organization handles and retains both information within and output from the information system in accordance with applicable federal laws, Executive Orders, directives, policies, regulations, standards, and operational requirements.

SI-13 PREDICTABLE FAILURE PREVENTION
Control: The organization:

a. Protects the information system from harm by considering mean time to failure for [Assignment: organization-defined list of information system components] in specific environments of operation; and

b. Provides substitute information system components, when needed, and a mechanism to exchange active and standby roles of the components.

ORGANIZATION-WIDE INFORMATION SECURITY PROGRAM MANAGEMENT CONTROLS

PM-1 INFORMATION SECURITY PROGRAM PLAN

Control: The organization:

a. Develops and disseminates an organization-wide information security program plan that:
- Provides an overview of the requirements for the security program and a description of the security program management controls and common controls in place or planned for meeting those requirements;
- Provides sufficient information about the program management controls and common controls (including specification of parameters for any assignment and selection operations either explicitly or by reference) to enable an implementation that is unambiguously compliant with the intent of the plan and a determination of the risk to be incurred if the plan is implemented as intended;
- Includes roles, responsibilities, management commitment, coordination among organizational entities, and compliance; and
- Is approved by a senior official with responsibility and accountability for the risk being incurred to organizational operations (including mission, functions, image, and reputation), organizational assets, individuals, other organizations, and the Nation;

b. Reviews the organization-wide information security program plan [Assignment: organization-defined frequency]; and

c. Revises the plan to address organizational changes and problems identified during plan implementation or security control assessments.

PM-2 SENIOR INFORMATION SECURITY OFFICER

Control: The organization appoints a senior information security officer with the mission and resources to coordinate, develop, implement, and maintain an organization-wide information security program.

PM-3 INFORMATION SECURITY RESOURCES

Control: The organization:

a. Ensures that all capital planning and investment requests include the resources needed to implement the information security program and documents all exceptions to this requirement;
b. Employs a business case/Exhibit 300/Exhibit 53 to record the resources required; and
c. Ensures that information security resources are available for expenditure as planned.

Supplemental Guidance: Organizations may designate and empower an Investment Review Board.

PM-4 PLAN OF ACTION AND MILESTONES PROCESS

Control: The organization implements a process for ensuring that plans of action and milestones for the security program and the associated organizational information systems are maintained and documents the remedial information security actions to mitigate risk to organizational operations and assets, individuals, other organizations, and the Nation.

PM-5 INFORMATION SYSTEM INVENTORY

Control: The organization develops and maintains an inventory of its information systems.

PM-6 INFORMATION SECURITY MEASURES OF PERFORMANCE

Control: The organization develops, monitors, and reports on the results of information security measures of performance.

PM-7 ENTERPRISE ARCHITECTURE

Control: The organization develops an enterprise architecture with consideration for information security and the resulting risk to organizational operations, organizational assets, individuals, other organizations, and the Nation.

PM-8 CRITICAL INFRASTRUCTURE PLAN

Control: The organization addresses information security issues in the development, documentation, and updating of a critical infrastructure and key resources protection plan.

PM-9 RISK MANAGEMENT STRATEGY

Control: The organization:

a. Develops a comprehensive strategy to manage risk to organizational operations and assets, individuals, other organizations, and the Nation associated with the operation and use of information systems; and
b. Implements that strategy consistently across the organization.

PM-10 SECURITY AUTHORIZATION PROCESS

Control: The organization:

a. Manages (i.e., documents, tracks, and reports) the security state of organizational information systems through security authorization processes;
b. Designates individuals to fulfill specific roles and responsibilities within the organizational risk management process; and
c. Fully integrates the security authorization processes into an organization-wide risk management program.

PM-11 MISSION/BUSINESS PROCESS DEFINITION

Control: The organization:

a. Defines mission/business processes with consideration for information security and the resulting risk to organizational operations, organizational assets, individuals, other organizations, and the Nation; and
b. Determines information protection needs arising from the defined mission/business processes and revises the processes as necessary, until an achievable set of protection needs is obtained.

Appendix C: HIPAA Security Rule

Administrative Safeguards

164.308(a)(1)(i)
Security Management Process: Implement policies and procedures to prevent, detect, contain, and correct security violations.

164.308(a)(1)(ii)(A)
Risk Analysis (R): Conduct an accurate and thorough assessment of the potential risks and vulnerabilities to the confidentiality, integrity, and availability of electronic protected health information held by the covered entity.

164.308(a)(1)(ii)(B)
Risk Management (R): Implement security measures sufficient to reduce risks and vulnerabilities to a reasonable and appropriate level to comply with Section 164.306(a).

164.308(a)(1)(ii)(C)
Sanction Policy (R): Apply appropriate sanctions against workforce members who fail to comply with the security policies and procedures of the covered entity.

164.308(a)(1)(ii)(D)
Information System Activity Review (R): Implement procedures to regularly review records of information system activity, such as audit logs, access reports, and security incident tracking reports.

164.308(a)(2)
Assigned Security Responsibility: Identify the security official who is responsible for the development and implementation of the policies and procedures required by this subpart for the entity.

164.308(a)(3)(i)
Workforce Security: Implement policies and procedures to ensure that all members of the workforce have appropriate access to electronic protected health information, as provided under paragraph (a)(4) of this section, and to prevent those workforce members who do not have access under paragraph (a)(4) of this section from obtaining access to electronic protected health information.

164.308(a)(3)(ii)(A)

Authorization and/or Supervision (A): Implement procedures for the authorization and/or supervision of workforce members who work with electronic protected health information or in locations where it might be accessed.

164.308(a)(3)(ii)(B)

Workforce Clearance Procedure (A): Implement procedures to determine that the access of a workforce member to electronic protected health information is appropriate.

164.308(a)(3)(ii)(C)

Termination Procedure (A): Implement procedures for terminating access to electronic protected health information when the employment of a workforce member ends or as required by determinations made as specified in paragraph (a)(3)(ii)(B) of this section.

164.308(a)(4)(i)

Information Access Management: Implement policies and procedures for authorizing access to electronic protected health information that are consistent with the applicable requirements of subpart E of this part.

164.308(a)(4)(ii)(A)

Isolating Healthcare Clearinghouse Functions (R): If a healthcare clearinghouse is part of a larger organization, the clearinghouse must implement policies and procedures that protect the electronic protected health information of the clearinghouse from unauthorized access by the larger organization.

164.308(a)(4)(ii)(B)

Access Authorization (A): Implement policies and procedures for granting access to electronic protected health information, for example, through access to a workstation, transaction, program, process, or other mechanism.

164.308(a)(4)(ii)(C)

Access Establishment and Modification (A): Implement policies and procedures that, based upon the entity's access authorization policies, establish, document, review, and modify a user's right of access to a workstation, transaction, program, or process.

164.308(a)(5)(i)

Security Awareness and Training: Implement a security awareness and training program for all members of the workforce (including management).

164.308(a)(5)(ii)(A)

Security Reminders (A): Periodic security updates.

164.308(a)(5)(ii)(B)

Protection from Malicious Software (A): Procedures for guarding against, detecting, and reporting malicious software.

164.308(a)(5)(ii)(C)

Log-in Monitoring (A): Procedures for monitoring log-in attempts and reporting discrepancies.

164.308(a)(5)(ii)(D)

Password Management (A): Procedures for creating, changing, and safeguarding passwords.

164.308(a)(6)(i)

Security Incident Procedures: Implement policies and procedures to address security incidents.

164.308(a)(6)(ii)

Response and Reporting (R): Identify and respond to suspected or known security incidents; mitigate, to the extent practicable, harmful effects of security incidents that are known to the covered entity; and document security incidents and their outcomes.

164.308(a)(7)(i)

Contingency Plan: Establish (and implement as needed) policies and procedures for responding to an emergency or other occurrence (for example, fire, vandalism, system failure, and natural disaster) that damages systems that contain electronic protected health information.

164.308(a)(7)(ii)(A)

Data Backup Plan (R): Establish and implement procedures to create and maintain retrievable exact copies of electronic protected health information.

164.308(a)(7)(ii)(B)

Disaster Recovery Plan (R): Establish (and implement as needed) procedures to restore any loss of data.

164.308(a)(7)(ii)(C)

Emergency Mode Operation Plan (R): Establish (and implement as needed) procedures to enable continuation of critical business processes for protection of the security of electronic protected health information while operating in emergency mode.

164.308(a)(7)(ii)(D)

Testing and Revision Procedure (A): Implement procedures for periodic testing and revision of contingency plans.

164.308(a)(7)(ii)(E)

Applications and Data Criticality Analysis (A): Assess the relative criticality of specific applications and data in support of other contingency plan components.

164.308(a)(8)

Evaluation: Perform a periodic technical and nontechnical evaluation, based initially upon the standards implemented under this rule and, subsequently, in response to environmental or operational changes affecting the security of electronic protected health information that establishes the extent to which an entity's security policies and procedures meet the requirements of this subpart.

164.308(b)(1)

Business Associate Contracts and Other Arrangements: A covered entity, in accordance with § 164.306, may permit a business associate to create, receive, maintain, or transmit electronic protected health information on the covered entity's behalf only if the covered entity obtains satisfactory assurances, in accordance with Sec. 164.314(a), that the business associate will appropriately safeguard the information.

164.308(b)(4)

Written Contract or Other Arrangement (R): Document the satisfactory assurances required by paragraph (b)(1) of this section through a written contract or other arrangement with the business associate that meets the applicable requirements of § 164.314(a).

Physical Safeguards

164.310(a)(1)

Facility Access Controls: Implement policies and procedures to limit physical access to electronic information systems and the facility or facilities in which they are housed, while ensuring that properly authorized access is allowed.

164.310(a)(2)(i)

Contingency Operations (A): Establish (and implement as needed) procedures that allow facility access in support of restoration of lost data under the disaster recovery plan and emergency mode operations plan in the event of an emergency.

164.310(a)(2)(ii)

Facility Security Plan (A): Implement policies and procedures to safeguard the facility and the equipment therein from unauthorized physical access, tampering, and theft.

164.310(a)(2)(iii)

Access Control and Validation Procedures (A): Implement procedures to control and validate a person's access to facilities based on his or her role or function, including visitor control, and control of access to software programs for testing and revision.

164.310(a)(2)(iv)

Maintenance Records (A): Implement policies and procedures to document repairs and modifications to the physical components of a facility that are related to security (for example, hardware, walls, doors, and locks).

164.310(b)

Workstation Use: Implement policies and procedures that specify the proper functions to be performed, the manner in which those functions are to be performed, and the physical attributes of the surroundings of a specific workstation or class of workstation that can access electronic protected health information.

164.310(c)

Workstation Security: Implement physical safeguards for all workstations that access electronic protected health information to restrict access to authorized users.

164.310(d)(1)
Device and Media Controls: Implement policies and procedures that govern the receipt and removal of hardware and electronic media that contain electronic protected health information into and out of a facility, and the movement of these items within the facility.

164.310(d)(2)(i)
Disposal (R): Implement policies and procedures to address the final disposition of electronic protected health information and/or the hardware or electronic media on which it is stored.

164.310(d)(2)(ii)
Media Reuse (R): Implement procedures for removal of electronic protected health information from electronic media before the media are made available for reuse.

164.310(d)(2)(iii)
Accountability (A): Maintain a record of the movements of hardware and electronic media and any person responsible therefore.

164.310(d)(2)(iv)
Data Backup and Storage (A): Create a retrievable exact copy of electronic protected health information, when needed, before movement of equipment.

Technical Safeguards
164.312(a)(1)
Access Control: Implement technical policies and procedures for electronic information systems that maintain electronic protected health information to allow access only to those persons or software programs that have been granted access rights as specified in § 164.308(a)(4).

164.312(a)(2)(i)
Unique User Identification (R): Assign a unique name and/or number for identifying and tracking user identity.

164.312(a)(2)(ii)
Emergency Access Procedure (R): Establish (and implement as needed) procedures for obtaining necessary electronic protected health information during an emergency.

164.312(a)(2)(iii)
Automatic Logoff (A): Implement electronic procedures that terminate an electronic session after a predetermined time of inactivity.

164.312(a)(2)(iv)
Encryption and Decryption (A): Implement a mechanism to encrypt and decrypt electronic protected health information.

164.312(b)
Audit Controls: Implement hardware, software, and/or procedural mechanisms that record and examine activity in information systems that contain or use electronic protected health information.

164.312(c)(1)
Integrity: Implement policies and procedures to protect electronic protected health information from improper alteration or destruction.

164.312(c)(2)
Mechanism to Authenticate Electronic Protected Health Information (A): Implement electronic mechanisms to corroborate that electronic protected health information has not been altered or destroyed in an unauthorized manner.

164.312(d)
Person or Entity Authentication: Implement procedures to verify that a person or entity seeking access to electronic protected health information is the one claimed.

164.312(e)(1)
Transmission Security: Implement technical security measures to guard against unauthorized access to electronic protected health information that is being transmitted over an electronic communications network.

164.312(e)(2)(i)
Integrity Controls: Implement security measures to ensure that electronically transmitted electronic protected health information is not improperly modified without detection until disposed of.

164.312(e)(2)(ii)
Encryption: Implement a mechanism to encrypt electronic protected health information whenever deemed appropriate.

Organizational

164.314(a)(1)

Business Associate Contracts or Other Arrangements:

(i) The contract or other arrangement between the covered entity and its business associate required by § 164.308(b) must meet the requirements of paragraph (a)(2)(i) or (a)(2)(ii) of this section, as applicable.

(ii) A covered entity is not in compliance with the standards in § 164.502(e) and paragraph (a) of this section if the covered entity knew of a pattern of an activity or practice of the business associate that constituted a material breach or violation of the business associate's obligation under the contract or other arrangement, unless the covered entity took reasonable steps to cure the breach or end the violation, as applicable, and, if such steps were unsuccessful, (A) terminated the contract or arrangement, if feasible; or (B) if termination is not feasible, reported the problem to the Secretary.

164.314(a)(2)(i)

Business Associate Contracts: The contract between a covered entity and a business associate must provide that the business associate will (A) implement administrative, physical, and technical safeguards that reasonably and appropriately protect the confidentiality, integrity, and availability of the electronic protected health information that it creates, receives, maintains, or transmits on behalf of the covered entity as required by this subpart; (B) ensure that any agent, including a subcontractor, to whom it provides such information agrees to implement reasonable and appropriate safeguards to protect it; (C) report to the covered entity any security incident of which it becomes aware; (D) authorize termination of the contract by the covered entity if the covered entity determines that the business associate has violated a material term of the contract.

164.314(a)(2)(ii)

Other Arrangements: When a covered entity and its business associate are both governmental entities, the covered entity is in compliance with paragraph (a)(1) of this section, if (1) it enters into a memorandum of understanding with the business associate that contains terms that accomplish the objectives of paragraph (a)(2)(i) of this section; or (2) other law (including regulations adopted by the covered entity or its business associate) contains requirements applicable to the business associate that accomplish the objectives of paragraph (a)(2)(i) of this section.

164.314(b)(1)

Requirements for Group Health Plans: Except when the only electronic protected health information disclosed to a plan sponsor is disclosed pursuant to § 164.504(f)(1)(ii) or (iii), or as authorized under § 164.508, a group health plan must ensure that its plan documents provide that the plan sponsor will reasonably and appropriately safeguard electronic protected health information created, received, maintained, or transmitted to or by the plan sponsor on behalf of the group health plan.

164.314(b)(2)(i)

Group Health Plan Implementation Specification: The plan documents of the group health plan must be amended to incorporate provisions to require the plan sponsor to (i) implement administrative, physical, and technical safeguards that reasonably and appropriately protect the confidentiality, integrity, and availability of the electronic protected health information that it creates, receives, maintains, or transmits on behalf of the group health plan.

164.314(b)(2)(ii)

Group Health Plan Implementation Specification: The plan documents of the group health plan must be amended to incorporate provisions to require the plan sponsor to (ii) ensure that the adequate separation required by § 164.504(f)(2)(iii) is supported by reasonable and appropriate security measures.

164.314(b)(2)(iii)

Group Health Plan Implementation Specification: The plan documents of the group health plan must be amended to incorporate provisions to require the plan sponsor to (iii) ensure that any agent, including a subcontractor, to whom it provides this information agrees to implement reasonable and appropriate security measures to protect the information.

164.314(b)(2)(iv)

Group Health Plan Implementation Specification: The plan documents of the group health plan must be amended to incorporate provisions to require the plan sponsor to (iv) report to the group health plan any security incident of which it becomes aware.

Policies and Procedure and Documentation Requirements

164.316(a)

Policies and Procedures: Implement reasonable and appropriate policies and procedures to comply with the standards, implementation specifications, or other requirements of this subpart, taking into account those factors specified in §164.306(b)(2)(i), (ii), (iii), and (iv). This standard is not to be construed to permit or excuse an action that violates any other standard, implementation specification, or other requirements of this subpart. A covered entity may change its policies and procedures at any time, provided that the changes are documented and are implemented in accordance with this subpart.

164.316(b)(1)

Documentation: (i) Maintain the policies and procedures implemented to comply with this subpart in written (which may be electronic) form; and (ii) if an action, activity, or assessment is required by this subpart to be documented, maintain a written (which may be electronic) record of the action, activity, or assessment.

164.316(b)(2)(i)

Time Limit: Retain the documentation required by paragraph (b)(1) of this section for 6 years from the date of its creation or the date when it last was in effect, whichever is later.

164.316(b)(2)(ii)

Availability: Make documentation available to those persons responsible for implementing the procedures to which the documentation pertains.

164.316(b)(2)(iii)

Updates: Review documentation periodically, and update as needed, in response to environmental or operational changes affecting the security of the electronic protected health information.

Appendix D: PCI DSS V2.0 Controls

Requirement 1—Install and Maintain Firewall Configuration to Maintain Data

1.1 Establish firewall and router configuration standards that include the following:

> 1.1.1 A formal process for approving and testing all network connections and changes to the firewall and router configurations
>
> 1.1.2 Current network diagram with all connections to cardholder data, including any wireless networks
>
> 1.1.3 Requirements for a firewall at each Internet connection and between any demilitarized zone (DMZ) and the internal network zone
>
> 1.1.4 Description of groups, roles, and responsibilities for logical management of network components
>
> 1.1.5 Documentation and business justification for use of all services, protocols, and ports allowed, including documentation of security features implemented for those protocols considered to be insecure
>
> Examples of insecure services, protocols, or ports include but are not limited to FTP, Telnet, POP3, IMAP, and SNMP.
>
> 1.1.6 Requirement to review firewall and router rule sets at least every 6 months

1.2 Build firewall and router configurations that restrict connections between untrusted networks and any system components in the cardholder data environment.

Note: An "untrusted network" is any network that is external to the networks belonging to the entity under review, and/or which is out of the entity's ability to control or manage.

> 1.2.1 Restrict inbound and outbound traffic to that which is necessary for the cardholder data environment.
>
> 1.2.2 Secure and synchronize router configuration files.
>
> 1.2.3 Install perimeter firewalls between any wireless networks and the cardholder data environment, and configure these

firewalls to deny or control (if such traffic is necessary for business purposes) any traffic from the wireless environment into the cardholder data environment.

1.3 Prohibit direct public access between the Internet and any system component in the cardholder data environment.

1.3.1 Implement a DMZ to limit inbound traffic to only system components that provide authorized publicly accessible services, protocols, and ports.

1.3.2 Limit inbound Internet traffic to IP addresses within the DMZ.

1.3.3 Do not allow any direct connections inbound or outbound for traffic between the Internet and the cardholder data environment.

1.3.4 Do not allow internal addresses to pass from the Internet into the DMZ.

1.3.5 Do not allow unauthorized outbound traffic from the cardholder data environment to the Internet.

1.3.6 Implement stateful inspection, also known as dynamic packet filtering. (That is, only "established" connections are allowed into the network.)

1.3.7 Place system components that store cardholder data (such as a database) in an internal network zone, segregated from the DMZ and other untrusted networks.

1.3.8 Do not disclose private IP addresses and routing information to unauthorized parties.

Note: Methods to obscure IP addressing may include, but are not limited to:

- Network address translation (NAT)
- Placing servers containing cardholder data behind proxy
- Servers/firewalls or content caches
- Removal or filtering of route advertisements for private networks that employ registered addressing
- Internal use of RFC1918 address space instead of registered addresses

1.4 Install personal firewall software on any mobile and/or employee-owned computers with direct connectivity to the Internet (for example, laptops used by employees), which are used to access the organization's network.

Requirement 2—Do Not Use Vendor-Supplied Defaults for Systems, Passwords, and Other Security Parameters

2.1 Always change vendor-supplied defaults before installing a system on the network, including but not limited to passwords, simple network management protocol (SNMP), community strings, and elimination of unnecessary accounts.

> 2.1.1 For wireless environments, connected to the cardholder data environment or transmitting cardholder data, change wireless vendor defaults, including but not limited to default wireless encryption keys, passwords, and SNMP community strings.

2.2 Develop configuration standards for all system components. Assure that these standards address all known security vulnerabilities and are consistent with industry-accepted system hardening standards. Sources of industry-accepted system hardening standards may include, but are not limited to:

- Center for Internet Security (CIS)
- International Organization for Standardization (ISO)
- SysAdmin Audit Network Security (SANS)
- National Institute of Standards Technology (NIST)

> 2.2.1 Implement only one primary function per server to prevent functions that require different security levels from coexisting on the same server. (For example, web servers, database servers, and DNS should be implemented on separate servers.)

Note: *Where virtualization technologies are in use, implement only one primary function per virtual system component.*

> 2.2.2 Enable only necessary and secure services, protocols, daemons, etc., as required for the function of the system. Implement security features for any required services, protocols, or daemons that are considered to be insecure—for example,

use secured technologies such as SSH, S-FTP, SSL, or IPSec VPN to protect insecure services such as NetBIOS, file sharing, Telnet, FTP, etc.

2.2.3 Configure system security parameters to prevent misuse.

2.2.4 Remove all unnecessary functionality, such as scripts, drivers, features, subsystems, file systems, and unnecessary web servers.

2.3 Encrypt all nonconsole administrative access using strong cryptography. Use technologies such as SSH, VPN, or SSL/TLS for web-based management and other nonconsole administrative access.

2.4 Shared-hosting providers must protect each entity's hosted environment and cardholder data. These providers must meet specific requirements as detailed in *Appendix A: Additional PCI DSS.*

Requirements for shared hosting providers

A.1.1 Ensure that each entity only runs processes that have access to that entity's cardholder data environment.

A.1.2 Restrict each entity's access and privileges to its own cardholder data environment only.

A.1.3 Ensure logging and audit trails are enabled and unique to each entity's cardholder data environment and consistent with PCI DSS Requirement 10.

A.1.4 Enable processes to provide for timely forensic investigation in the event of a compromise to any hosted merchant or service provider.

Requirement 3—Protect Stored Cardholder Data

3.1 Keep cardholder data storage to a minimum by implementing data retention and disposal policies, procedures, and processes, as follows:

3.1.1 Implement a data retention and disposal policy that includes:
- Limiting data storage amount and retention time to that which is required for legal, regulatory, and business requirements
- Processes for secure deletion of data when no longer needed
- Specific retention requirements for cardholder data

- A quarterly automatic or manual process for identifying and securely deleting stored cardholder data that exceeds defined retention requirements

3.2 Do not store sensitive authentication data after authorization (even if encrypted). Sensitive authentication data include the data as cited in the following Requirements 3.2.1 through 3.2.3.

Note: *It is permissible for issuers and companies that support issuing services to store sensitive authentication data if there is a business justification and the data is stored securely.*

3.2.1 Do not store the full contents of any track (from the magnetic stripe located on the back of a card, equivalent data contained on a chip, or elsewhere). These data are alternatively called full track, track, track 1, track 2, and magnetic-stripe data.

Note: *In the normal course of business, the following data elements from the magnetic stripe may need to be retained:*

- The cardholder's name
- Primary account number (PAN)
- Expiration date
- Service code (To minimize risk, store only these data elements as needed for business.)

3.2.2 Do not store the card verification code or value (three-digit or four-digit number printed on the front or back of a payment card) used to verify card-not-present transactions.

3.2.3 Do not store the personal identification number (PIN) or the encrypted PIN block.

3.3 Mask PAN when displayed (the first six and last four digits are the maximum number of digits to be displayed)

Notes:

- This requirement does not apply to employees and other parties with a legitimate business need to see the full PAN.
- This requirement does not supersede stricter requirements in place for displays of cardholder data—for example, for point-of-sale (POS) receipts.

3.4 Render PAN unreadable anywhere it is stored (including on portable digital media, backup media, and in logs) by using any of the following approaches:

- One-way hashes based on strong cryptography (hash must be of the entire PAN)
- Truncation (hashing cannot be used to replace the truncated segment of PAN)
- Index tokens and pads (pads must be securely stored)
- Strong cryptography with associated key-management processes and procedures

Note: It is a relatively trivial effort for a malicious individual to reconstruct original PAN data if he or she has access to both the truncated and hashed versions of a PAN. Where hashed and truncated versions of the same PAN are present in an entity's environment, additional controls should be in place to ensure that the hashed and truncated versions cannot be correlated to reconstruct the original PAN.

3.4.1 If disk encryption is used (rather than file- or column-level database encryption), logical access must be managed independently of native operating system access control mechanisms (for example, by not using local user account databases). Decryption keys must not be tied to user accounts.

3.5 Protect any keys used to secure cardholder data against disclosure and misuse:

Note: This requirement also applies to key-encrypting keys used to protect data-encrypting keys—such key-encrypting keys must be at least as strong as the data-encrypting key.

3.5.1 Restrict access to cryptographic keys to the fewest number of custodians necessary.

3.5.2 Store cryptographic keys securely in the fewest possible locations and forms.

3.6 Fully document and implement all key-management processes and procedures for cryptographic keys used for encryption of cardholder data, including the following.

Note: *Numerous industry standards for key management are available from various resources including NIST, which can be found at* http://csrc.nist.gov.

3.6.1 Generation of strong cryptographic keys

3.6.2 Secure cryptographic key distribution

3.6.3 Secure cryptographic key storage

3.6.4 Cryptographic key changes for keys that have reached the end of their cryptoperiod (for example, after a defined period of time has passed and/or after a certain amount of ciphertext has been produced by a given key), as defined by the associated application vendor or key owner, and based on industry best practices and guidelines (for example, NIST Special Publication 800-57)

3.6.5 Retirement or replacement (for example, archiving, destruction, and/or revocation) of keys as deemed necessary when the integrity of the key has been weakened (for example, departure of an employee with knowledge of a clear-text key) or keys are suspected of being compromised

Note: *If retired or replaced cryptographic keys need to be retained, these keys must be securely archived (for example, by using a key-encryption key). Archived cryptographic keys should only be used for decryption/verification purposes.*

3.6.6 If manual clear-text cryptographic key management operations are used, these operations must be managed using split knowledge and dual control (for example, requiring two or three people, each knowing only their own key component, to reconstruct the whole key).

Note: *Examples of manual key management operations include, but are not limited to: key generation, transmission, loading, storage, and destruction.*

3.6.7 Prevention of unauthorized substitution of cryptographic keys

3.6.8 Requirement for cryptographic key custodians to formally acknowledge that they understand and accept their key-custodian responsibilities

Requirement 4—Encrypt Transmission of Cardholder Data across Open, Public Networks

4.1 Use strong cryptography and security protocols (for example, SSL/TLS, IPSEC, SSH, etc.) to safeguard sensitive cardholder data during transmission over open, public networks.

Examples of open, public networks that are in scope of the PCI DSS include but are not limited to:

- The Internet
- Wireless technologies
- Global system for mobile communications (GSM)
- General packet radio service (GPRS)

4.1.1 Ensure that wireless networks transmitting cardholder data or connected to the cardholder data environment use industry best practices (for example, IEEE 802.11i) to implement strong encryption for authentication and transmission.

Note: *The use of WEP as a security control was prohibited as of June 30, 2010.*

4.2 Never send unencrypted PANs by end-user messaging technologies (for example, e-mail, instant messaging, chat, etc.).

Requirement 5—Vulnerability Management Program
5.1 Deploy antivirus software on all systems commonly affected by malicious software (particularly personal computers and servers).

5.1.1 Ensure that all antivirus programs are capable of detecting, removing, and protecting against all known types of malicious software.

5.2 Ensure that all antivirus mechanisms are current, actively running, and capable of generating audit logs.

Requirement 6—Develop and Maintain Secure Systems and Applications
6.1 Ensure that all system components and software are protected from known vulnerabilities by having the latest vendor-supplied security patches installed. Install critical security patches within 1 month of release.

Note: *An organization may consider applying a risk-based approach to prioritize patch installations—for example, by prioritizing critical infrastructure (for example, public-facing devices and systems, databases) higher than less critical internal devices to ensure high-priority systems and devices are addressed within 1 month, and addressing less critical devices and systems within 3 months.*

6.2 Establish a process to identify and assign a risk ranking to newly discovered security vulnerabilities.

Notes:

- Risk rankings should be based on industry best practices. For example, criteria for ranking "high" risk vulnerabilities may include a CVSS base score of 4.0 or above, and/or a vendor-supplied patch classified by the vendor as "critical," and/or a vulnerability affecting a critical system component.
- The ranking of vulnerabilities as defined in 6.2.a is considered a best practice until June 30, 2012, after which it becomes a requirement.

6.3 Develop software applications (internal and external, and including web-based administrative access to applications) in accordance with PCI DSS (for example, secure authentication and logging) and based on industry best practices. Incorporate information security throughout the software development life cycle. These processes must include the following:

6.3.1 Removal of custom application accounts, user IDs, and passwords before applications become active or are released to customers

6.3.2 Review of custom code prior to release to production or customers in order to identify any potential coding vulnerability

6.4 Follow change control processes and procedures for all changes to system components. The procedures must include the following:

6.4.1 Separate development/test and production environments.

6.4.2 Separate duties between development/test and production environments.

6.4.3 Production data (live PANs) are not used for testing or development.

6.4.4 Remove test data and accounts before production systems become active.

6.4.5 Change control procedures for the implementation of security patches and software modifications must include the following:

6.4.5.1 Documentation of impact

6.4.5.2 Documented change approval by authorized parties

6.4.5.3 Functionality testing to verify that the change does not adversely impact the security of the system

6.4.5.4 Back-out procedures

6.5 Develop applications based on secure coding guidelines. Prevent common coding vulnerabilities in software development processes, to include the following.

Note: *The vulnerabilities listed at 6.5.1 through 6.5.9 were current with industry best practices when this version of PCI DSS was published. However, as industry best practices for vulnerability management are updated (for example, the OWASP Guide, SANS CWE Top 25, CERT Secure Coding, etc.), the current best practices must be used for these requirements.*

6.5.1 Injection flaws, particularly SQL injection. Also consider OS Command Injection, LDAP, and XPath injection flaws as well as other injection flaws.

6.5.2 Buffer overflow

6.5.3 Insecure cryptographic storage

6.5.4 Insecure communications

6.5.5 Improper error handling

6.5.6 All "high" vulnerabilities identified in the vulnerability identification process (as defined in PCI DSS Requirement 6.2)

Note: *This requirement is considered a best practice until June 30, 2012, after which it becomes a requirement.*

6.5.7 Cross-site scripting (XSS)

6.5.8 Improper access control (such as insecure direct object references, failure to restrict URL access, and directory traversal)

6.5.9 Cross-site request forgery (CSRF)

6.6 For public-facing web applications, address new threats and vulnerabilities on an ongoing basis and ensure these applications are protected against known attacks by *either* of the following methods:

- Reviewing public-facing web applications via manual or automated application vulnerability security assessment tools or methods, at least annually and after any changes
- Installing a web-application firewall in front of public-facing web applications

Requirement 7—Restrict Access to Cardholder Data by Business Need to Know

7.1 Limit access to system components and cardholder data to only those individuals whose job requires such access. Access limitations must include the following:

> 7.1.1 Restriction of access rights to privileged user IDs to least privileges necessary to perform job responsibilities
>
> 7.1.2 Assignment of privileges based on individual personnel's job classification and function
>
> 7.1.3 Requirement for a documented approval by authorized parties specifying required privileges
>
> 7.1.4 Implementation of an automated access control system

7.2 Establish an access control system for systems components with multiple users that restricts access based on a user's need to know and is set to "deny all" unless specifically allowed. This access control system must include the following:

> 7.2.1 Coverage of all system components
>
> 7.2.2 Assignment of privileges to individuals based on job classification and function
>
> 7.2.3 Default "deny-all" setting
>
> **Note:** *Some access control systems are set by default to "allow-all," thereby permitting access unless/until a rule is written to specifically deny it.*

Requirement 8—Assign a Unique ID to Each Person with Computer Access

8.1 Assign all users a unique ID before allowing them to access system components or cardholder data.

8.2 In addition to assigning a unique ID, employ at least one of the following methods to authenticate all users:

- Something you know, such as a password or passphrase
- Something you have, such as a token device or smart card
- Something you are, such as a biometric

8.3 Incorporate two-factor authentication for remote access (network-level access originating from outside the network) to the network by employees, administrators, and third parties (for example, remote authentication and dial-in service [RADIUS] with tokens; terminal access controller access control system [TACACS] with tokens; or other technologies that facilitate two-factor authentication).

Note: *Two-factor authentication requires that two of the three authentication methods (see Requirement 8.2 for descriptions of authentication methods) be used for authentication. Using one factor twice (for example, using two separate passwords) is not considered two-factor authentication.*

8.4 Render all passwords unreadable during transmission and storage on all system components using strong cryptography.

8.5 Ensure proper user identification and authentication management for nonconsumer users and administrators on all system components as follows:

8.5.1 Control addition, deletion, and modification of user IDs, credentials, and other identifier objects.

8.5.2 Verify user identity before performing password resets.

8.5.3 Set passwords for first-time use and resets to a unique value for each user and change immediately after the first use.

8.5.4 Immediately revoke access for any terminated users.

8.5.5 Remove/disable inactive user accounts at least every 90 days.

8.5.6 Enable accounts used by vendors for remote access only during the time period needed. Monitor vendor remote access accounts when in use.

8.5.7 Communicate authentication procedures and policies to all users who have access to cardholder data.

8.5.8 Do not use group, shared, or generic accounts and passwords or other authentication methods.

8.5.9 Change user passwords at least every 90 days.

8.5.10 Require a minimum password length of at least seven characters.

8.5.11 Use passwords containing both numeric and alphabetic characters.

8.5.12 Do not allow an individual to submit a new password that is the same as any of the last four passwords he or she has used.

8.5.13 Limit repeated access attempts by locking out the user ID after not more than six attempts.

8.5.14 Set the lockout duration to a minimum of 30 minutes or until the administrator enables the user ID.

8.5.15 If a session has been idle for more than 15 minutes, require the user to reauthenticate to reactivate the terminal or session.

8.5.16 Authenticate all access to any database containing cardholder data. This includes access by applications, administrators, and all other users. Restrict user direct access or queries to databases to database administrators.

Requirement 9—Restrict Physical Access to Cardholder Data

9.1 Use video cameras and/or access control mechanisms to monitor individual physical access to sensitive areas. Review collected data and correlate with other entries. Store for at least 3 months, unless otherwise restricted by law.

Note: *"Sensitive areas" refers to any data center, server room, or any area that houses systems that store, process, or transmit cardholder data. This excludes the areas where only point-of-sale terminals are present, such as the cashier areas in a retail store.*

9.1.1 Use video cameras and/or access control mechanisms to monitor individual physical access to sensitive areas. Review collected data and correlate with other entries. Store for at least 3 months, unless otherwise restricted by law.

9.1.2 Restrict physical access to publicly accessible network jacks. For example, areas accessible to visitors should not have network ports enabled unless network access is explicitly authorized.

9.1.3 Restrict physical access to wireless access points, gateways, handheld devices, networking/communications hardware, and telecommunication lines.

9.2 Develop procedures to easily distinguish between onsite personnel and visitors, especially in areas where cardholder data are accessible.

9.3 Make sure all visitors are handled as follows:

9.3.1 Authorized before entering areas where cardholder data are processed or maintained

9.3.2 Given a physical token (for example, a badge or access device) that expires and that identifies the visitors as not onsite personnel

9.3.3 Asked to surrender the physical token before leaving the facility or at the date of expiration

9.4 Use a visitor log to maintain a physical audit trail of visitor activity. Document the visitor's name, the firm represented, and the onsite personnel authorizing physical access on the log. Retain this log for a minimum of 3 months, unless otherwise restricted by law.

9.5 Store media backups in a secure location, preferably an off-site facility, such as an alternate or backup site, or a commercial storage facility. Review the location's security at least annually.

9.6 Physically secure all media.

9.7 Maintain strict control over the internal or external distribution of any kind of media, including the following:

9.7.1 Classify media so that the sensitivity of the data can be determined.

9.7.2 Send the media by secured courier or other delivery method that can be accurately tracked.

9.8 Ensure that management approves any and all media containing cardholder data that are moved from a secured area (especially when media are distributed to individuals).

9.9 Maintain strict control over the storage and accessibility of media.

9.9.1 Properly maintain inventory logs of all media and conduct media inventories at least annually.

9.10 Destroy media when they are no longer needed for business or legal reasons as follows:

9.10.1 Shred, incinerate, or pulp hardcopy materials so that cardholder data cannot be reconstructed.

9.10.2 Render cardholder data on electronic media unrecoverable so that cardholder data cannot be reconstructed.

Requirement 10—Track and Monitor All Access to Network Resources and Cardholder Data

10.1 Establish a process for linking all access to system components (especially access done with administrative privileges such as root) to each individual user.

10.2 Implement automated audit trails for all system components to reconstruct the following events:

10.2.1 All individual accesses to cardholder data

10.2.2 All actions taken by any individual with root or administrative privileges

10.2.3 Access to all audit trails

10.2.4 Invalid logical access attempts

10.2.5 Use of identification and authentication mechanisms

10.2.6 Initialization of the audit logs

10.2.7 Creation and deletion of system-level objects

10.3 Record at least the following audit trail entries for all system components for each event:

10.3.1 User identification

10.3.2 Type of event

10.3.3 Date and time

10.3.4 Success or failure indication

10.3.5 Origination of event

10.3.6 Identity or name of affected data, system component, or resource

10.4 Using time-synchronization technology, synchronize all critical system clocks and times and ensure that the following is implemented for acquiring, distributing, and storing time.

Note: *One example of time synchronization technology is network time protocol (NTP).*

10.4.1 Critical systems have the correct and consistent time.

10.4.2 Time data are protected.

10.4.3 Time settings are received from industry-accepted time sources.

10.5 Secure audit trails so that they cannot be altered.

10.5.1 Limit viewing of audit trails to those with a job-related need.

10.5.2 Protect audit trail files from unauthorized modifications.

10.5.3 Promptly back up audit trail files to a centralized log server or media that are difficult to alter.

10.5.4 Write logs for external-facing technologies onto a log server on the internal LAN.

10.5.5 Use file-integrity monitoring or change-detection software on logs to ensure that existing log data cannot be changed without generating alerts (although new data being added should not cause an alert).

10.6 Review logs for all system components at least daily. Log reviews must include those servers that perform security functions like intrusion-detection system (IDS) and authentication, authorization, and accounting (AAA) protocol servers (for example, RADIUS).

Note: *Log harvesting, parsing, and alerting tools may be used to meet compliance with Requirement 10.6.*

10.7 Retain audit trail history for at least 1 year, with a minimum of 3 months immediately available for analysis (for example, online, archived, or restorable from backup).

Requirement 11—Regularly Test Security Systems and Processes
11.1 Test for the presence of wireless access points and detect unauthorized wireless access points on a quarterly basis.

Note: *Methods that may be used in the process include but are not limited to wireless network scans, physical/logical inspections of system components and infrastructure, network access control (NAC), or wireless IDS/IPS. Whichever methods are used, they must be sufficient to detect and identify any unauthorized devices.*

11.2 Run internal and external network vulnerability scans at least quarterly and after any significant change in the network (such as new system component installations, changes in network topology, firewall rule modifications, product upgrades).

Note: *It is not required that four passing quarterly scans must be completed for initial PCI DSS compliance if the assessor verifies that (1) the most recent scan result was a passing scan, (2) the entity has documented policies and procedures requiring quarterly scanning, and (3) vulnerabilities noted in the scan results have been corrected as shown in a rescan. For subsequent years after the initial PCI DSS review, four passing quarterly scans must have occurred.*

11.2.1 Perform quarterly internal vulnerability scans.

11.2.2 Perform quarterly external vulnerability scans via an approved scanning vendor (ASV), approved by the Payment Card Industry Security Standards Council (PCI SSC).

Note: *Quarterly external vulnerability scans must be performed by an ASV, approved by PCI SSC. Scans conducted after network changes may be performed by internal staff.*

11.2.3 Perform internal and external scans after any significant change.

Note: *Scans conducted after changes may be performed by internal staff.*

11.3 Perform external and internal penetration testing at least once a year and after any significant infrastructure or application upgrade or modification (such as an operating system upgrade, a subnetwork added to the environment, or a web server added to the environment). These penetration tests must include the following:

11.3.1 Network-layer penetration tests

11.3.2 Application-layer penetration tests

11.4 Use intrusion-detection systems and/or intrusion-prevention systems to monitor all traffic at the perimeter of the cardholder data environment as well as at critical points inside the cardholder data environment, and alert personnel to suspected compromises. Keep all intrusion-detection and prevention engines, baselines, and signatures up to date.

11.5 Deploy file-integrity monitoring tools to alert personnel to unauthorized modification of critical system files, configuration files, or content files; configure the software to perform critical file comparisons at least weekly.

Note: *For file-integrity monitoring purposes, critical files are usually those that do not regularly change, but the modification of which could indicate a system compromise or risk of compromise. File-integrity monitoring products usually come preconfigured with critical files for the related operating system. Other critical files, such as those for custom applications, must be evaluated and defined by the entity (that is, the merchant or service provider).*

Requirement 12—Maintain a Policy That Addresses Information Security for Employees and Contractors

12.1 Establish, publish, maintain, and disseminate a security policy that accomplishes the following:

   12.1.1 Addresses all PCI DSS requirements

   12.1.2 Includes an annual process that identifies threats and vulnerabilities and results in a formal risk assessment (Examples of risk assessment methodologies include but are not limited to OCTAVE, ISO 27005, and NIST SP 800-30.)

   12.1.3 Includes a review at least annually and updates when the environment changes

12.2 Develop daily operational security procedures that are consistent with requirements in this specification (for example, user account maintenance procedures and log review procedures).

12.3 Develop usage policies for critical technologies (for example, remote-access technologies, wireless technologies, removable electronic media, laptops, personal data/digital assistants (PDAs), e-mail usage, and Internet usage) and define proper use of these technologies. Ensure that these usage policies require the following:

   12.3.1 Explicit management approval

   12.3.2 Authentication for use of the technology

   12.3.3 A list of all such devices and personnel with access

   12.3.4 Labeling of devices to determine owner, contact information, and purpose

   12.3.5 Acceptable uses of the technology

   12.3.6 Acceptable network locations for the technologies

   12.3.7 List of company-approved products

   12.3.8 Automatic disconnect of sessions for remote-access technologies after a specific period of inactivity

   12.3.9 Activation of remote-access technologies for vendors and business partners only when needed by vendors and business partners, with immediate deactivation after use

   12.3.10 For personnel accessing cardholder data via remote-access technologies, prohibition of copy, move, and storage of cardholder data onto local hard drives and removable electronic media, unless explicitly authorized for a defined business need

12.4 Ensure that the security policy and procedures clearly define information security responsibilities for all personnel.

12.5 Assign to an individual or team the following information security management responsibilities:

12.5.1 Establish, document, and distribute security policies and procedures.

12.5.2 Monitor and analyze security alerts and information, and distribute to appropriate personnel.

12.5.3 Establish, document, and distribute security incident response and escalation procedures to ensure timely and effective handling of all situations.

12.5.4 Administer user accounts, including additions, deletions, and modifications.

12.5.5 Monitor and control all access to data.

12.6 Implement a formal security awareness program to make all employees aware of the importance of cardholder data security.

12.6.1 Educate personnel upon hire and at least annually.

Note: *Methods can vary depending on the role of the personnel and their level of access to the cardholder data.*

12.6.2 Require personnel to acknowledge at least annually that they have read and understood the security policy and procedures.

12.7 Screen potential personnel prior to hire to minimize the risk of attacks from internal sources. (Examples of background checks include previous employment history, criminal record, credit history, and reference checks.)

Note: *For those potential personnel to be hired for certain positions, such as store cashiers who only have access to one card number at a time when facilitating a transaction, this requirement is a recommendation only.*

12.8 If cardholder data are shared with service providers, maintain and implement policies and procedures to manage service providers, to include the following:

12.8.1 Maintain a list of service providers.

12.8.2 Maintain a written agreement that includes an acknowledgment that the service providers are responsible for the security of cardholder data that the service providers possess.

12.8.3 Ensure that there is an established process for engaging service providers, including proper due diligence prior to engagement.

12.8.4 Maintain a program to monitor service providers' PCI DSS compliance status at least annually.

12.9 Implement an incident response plan. Be prepared to respond immediately to a system breach.

12.9.1 Create the incident response plan to be implemented in the event of system breach. Ensure the plan addresses the following, at a minimum:
- Roles, responsibilities, and communication and contact strategies in the event of a compromise, including notification of the payment brands, at a minimum
- Specific incident response procedures
- Business recovery and continuity procedures
- Data backup processes
- Analysis of legal requirements for reporting compromises
- Coverage and responses of all critical system components
- Reference or inclusion of incident response procedures from the payment brands

12.9.2 Test the plan at least annually.

12.9.3 Designate specific personnel to be available on a 24/7 basis to respond to alerts.

12.9.4 Provide appropriate training to staff with security breach response responsibilities.

12.9.5 Include alerts from intrusion-detection, intrusion-prevention, and file-integrity monitoring systems.

12.9.6 Develop process to modify and evolve the incident response plan according to lessons learned and to incorporate industry developments.

Appendix E: Agreed-Upon Procedures (AUPs) V5.0

A. Risk Management

A.1 A formal risk governance program is implemented.

A.2 A formal risk governance program is aligned with the business environment.

B. Information Security Policy

B.1 An information security policy is maintained that includes the key relevant domains of security.

B.2 An organization should review the information security policy at planned intervals, at least annually (or if significant changes occur), to ensure its continuing suitability, adequacy, and effectiveness.

B.3 Employees signify their acceptance of the company's acceptable use policy at least annually.

C. Organization of Information Security

C.1 An organization should communicate, get acknowledgment from, and periodically review employees' responsibility to protect confidential information. Employees must acknowledge this communication by signing a confidentiality agreement.

C.2 Dependent service provider agreements detail security requirements between the service provider and the dependent service provider.

D. Asset Management

D.1 An inventory of all assets is maintained with required information.

E. Human Resources Security

E.1 Security awareness training occurs at least annually and attendance reports for employees are maintained.

E.2 Background investigation policy includes relevant industry security examination requirements.

F. Physical and Environmental Security

F.1 An organization should ensure that critical supporting utilities, such as climate control, fire suppressants, and backup power supplies, needed to support the business are in place.

F.2 Target data, target systems, and physical media are protected with physical security controls.

F.3 The controls in the secure work space are commensurate with the risk and are part of the organization's security and risk management program.

F.4 Organizations should control ingress into and egress out of the secure workspace.

F.5 Access to secure work place is logged and incident reports are maintained.

F.6 Periodic compliance audits of the secure work space environment are conducted.

G. Communications and Operations Management

G.1 Signatures are up to date on network intrusion detection systems (IDS)/intrusion prevention sensors (IPS).

G.2 Authentication credentials transmitted to network devices are encrypted in transit.

G.3 High-risk administrative ports on externally facing target systems are not accessible from the Internet.

G.4 Network connections are logged and the log files are retained for examination.

G.5 Virus signature files are up to date for target servers.

G.6 Virus signature files are up to date for target workstations.

G.7 Systems and network logging is enabled and system audit log files are retained.

G.8 Key log attributes are logged and reported in the system audit log files.

G.9 Audit logs are retained for the required duration.

G.10 A privacy policy exists on Internet-facing websites from the point where end users access target data.

G.11 SSL authentication and encryption are enabled.

G.12 E-mail relaying is disabled.

G.13 Tracking is in place for physical media used for transporting target data from preshipment until destruction.

G.14 Backup media containing target data from target systems are transported off-site in a lockbox.

G.15 Only prior approved wireless access points are present on the network.

G.16 Encryption and authentication are required prior to connecting to internal wireless access points.

G.17 Firewalls protect and are inspecting traffic between defined network zones that possess different levels of trust.

G.18 Network rules are authorized.

G.19 IDS/IPS alert events contain required security information.

G.20 Backups occur and are restored successfully.

G.21 A formal change request process is in place and change requests are documented, tested, and approved prior to implementation.

H. Access Control

H.1 Password security settings on each system are implemented.

H.2 User system access is removed upon termination.

H.3 An approval process exists for logical access requests.

H.4 Inactive accounts are locked or disabled.

H.5 Unattended systems are locked.

H.6 User access to facilities where target systems reside is removed upon termination.

H.7 Physical access is authorized.

H.8 Multifactor authentication is required for staff administrator remote access.

I. Information Systems Acquisition, Development, and Maintenance

I.1 Vulnerability assessments are performed on externally facing proprietary website applications that process, store, or transmit target data.

I.2 Secure SDLC code reviews are performed on externally facing proprietary website applications that process, store, or transmit target data.

I.3 Secure systems configuration standards include required industry best practices.

I.4 System patches are applied.

I.5 A formal application security risk governance program is implemented.

I.6 Application risks are assessed as part of a formal application security vulnerability assessment and remediation program.

I.7 Security reviews are completed within the organization's SDLC program.

I.8 Security reviews are performed on internally developed applications and third-party applications that process, store, or transmit target data.

I.9 Application security awareness course content deals with security vulnerabilities and is applicable to the organization and its environment.

I.10 Developers attend application security awareness training annually and pass an application security exam upon course completion.

J. Information Security Incident Management

J.1 Information security incident management policy and procedures incorporate key relevant attributes.

K. Business Continuity Management

K.1 Business impact analysis is implemented.

K.2 BIA is aligned with existing assets and the key industry threats to these are identified.

K.3 A business continuity governance plan is implemented and maintained.

K.4 A business process level analysis and plan is implemented and maintained.

K.5 A threat assessment is conducted based on the actual threat environment, the nature of the service provided, and the service provision environment.

K.6 Business continuity test plans for business processes are scoped, and the problems identified are made visible and have an associated remediation action.

L. Compliance

L.1 Log-on banners are presented at log-on, informing users of restrictions.

L.2 Target systems are scanned for vulnerabilities and identified vulnerabilities are remediated.

P. Management of Privacy Program

P.1 An inventory of all target privacy data, defined by data subject category, its ownership, and its flow, is maintained and updated annually with all required information in the privacy inventory/flow. It has been approved and reviewed within the last 12 months and contains a revision history.

P.2 Privacy policy and privacy notices of service provider and third parties have been developed, are maintained, include the privacy principles developed by the OECD or the generally accepted privacy principles developed by the AICPA/CICA, have been approved and reviewed within the last 12 months, and contain a revision history.

P.3 An individual has been assigned as accountable for the privacy program at service providers and third parties. Accountability includes creation, review, enforcement, and a change management process for the privacy policy and program. This responsibility is documented as part of the organization chart and roles and responsibilities for the privacy program. Key procedures have been written for due diligence, review and compliance, enforcement and monitoring, and change management.

P.4 Privacy agreements detail privacy and protection requirements between the service provider and its third parties that have access to target privacy data.

P.5 A record is maintained of all required notifications, registrations, permits, approvals, adequacy mechanisms, and reviews/approvals from any mandated entities (such as employee-related bodies, councils, or unions) of the privacy policy.

P.6 Privacy procedures, which include the key relevant domains of privacy, are enforced and maintained.

P.7 Privacy awareness training occurs at least annually and during on-boarding of new employees, addressing a broad set of privacy topics with comprehension testing included. Attendance reports for service provider employees and third-party employees are maintained.

P.8 Privacy communication procedures incorporate key relevant attributes of current communications regarding privacy communications, suspected issues, breach management laws, regulation, and policy.